my gluten-free kitchen

my
gluten-free
kitchen

Gearóid Lynch

Gill Books

Gill Books
Hume Avenue
Park West
Dublin 12
www.gillbooks.ie

Gill Books is an imprint of M. H. Gill & Co.

© Gearóid Lynch 2016

978 07171 6990 0

Designed by www.grahamthew.com
Edited by Kristin Jensen
Photography © Joanne Murphy www.joanne-murphy.com
Styled by Orla Neligan of Cornershop Productions
www.cornershopproductions.com
Stylist's assistant: Louise O'Leary
Indexed by Adam Pozner
Printed by Liberdúplex, Spain

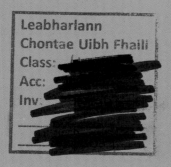
Props

Avoca: HQ Kilmacanogue, Bray, Co. Wicklow.
T: (01) 2746939; E: info@avoca.ie; www.avoca.ie
Meadows & Byrne: Dublin, Cork, Galway, Clare, Tipperary.
T: (01) 2804554/(021) 4344100;
E: info@meadowsandbyrne.ie; www.meadowsandbyrne.com
Marks & Spencer: Unit 1–28, Dundrum Town Centre,
Dublin 16. T: (01) 2991300; www.marksandspencer.ie
Article Dublin: Powerscourt Townhouse, South William
Street, Dublin 2. T: (01) 6799268;
E: items@articledublin.com; www.articledublin.com
Dunnes Stores: 46–50 South Great George's Street, Dublin 2.
T: 1890 253185; www.dunnesstores.com
Harold's Bazaar: 208 Harold's Cross Road, Dublin 6W.
T: 087 7228789.
Historic Interiors: Oberstown, Lusk, Co. Dublin.
T: (01) 8437174; E: killian@historicinteriors.net
TK Maxx: The Park, Carrickmines, Dublin 18. T: 01 2074798;
www.tkmaxx.ie
Golden Biscotti ceramics: www.goldenbiscotti.bigcartel.com
The Patio Centre: The Hill Centre, Johnstown Road,
Glenageary, Cabinteely, Dublin 18. T: (01) 2350714;
thepatiocentre.com
Industry Design: 41 A/B Drury Street, Dublin 2.
T: (01) 6139111; www.industrydesign.ie
Maddocks: Thornhill Road, Fassaroe, Bray, Co. Wicklow.
T: (01) 2868418; www.maddocksbray.ie

This book is typeset in 10 on 13.5pt Mercury.

*The paper used in this book comes from the wood pulp of
managed forests. For every tree felled, at least one tree is
planted, thereby renewing natural resources.*

A CIP catalogue record for this book is available from the
British Library.

5 4 3 2 1

In 2002 **Gearóid Lynch** and his wife, Tara, purchased the historic post-house building in Cloverhill, Co. Cavan and lovingly restored it to its original charm. Together, they run The Olde Post Inn alongside their dedicated team, and it has become an award-winning food destination lauded by food critics and loyal customers alike. Since his diagnosis with coeliac disease in 2013, Gearóid has adapted the majority of his menus for gluten-free diners in his restaurant. Gearóid trained as a chef in Killybegs Tourism College and gained experience working in kitchens, such as Thornton's and Le Coq Hardi in Dublin, as well as restaurants in London and Luxembourg. He is a regular contributor to national media and a highly respected chef in culinary circles, having been appointed to the role of Commissioner General with Eurotoques Ireland in 2011 for a two-year period. From Co. Cavan, Gearóid and Tara live locally with their four children, Orán, Lorcan, Emma and Eoin.

acknowledgements

I would first like to thank Deirdre Nolan and Sarah Liddy at Gill Books for the opportunity to write this cookbook. They both had great faith in me – I think it was the wild garlic bread that won them over! Thanks also to Catherine Gough, Teresa Daly and Emma Lynam at Gill Books for all their help.

Thanks to Joanne Murphy for her great eye and attention to detail and to Orla Neligan for her great style and taste. Both are a pleasure to work with.

To Kristin Jensen, many thanks for your patience and professionalism and complete love of fresh herbs!

Thank you to Bridget O'Dea from Purcell Masterson and all the team. You are a cracker and a great support who is always there for me.

Thank you to The Olde Post Inn team for all your support from the get-go, especially to Garrett Galligan, who was cracking the whip and without whom I could not have put this book together. The truly gifted pastry chef that is Brid Teevan tirelessly retried recipes for me again and again. I am truly blessed to be working with her.

To Catherine Fox, thank you for the dig-out with the typing and sampling. Thanks also to David Molloy in DT One Menswear in Cavan.

I'm delighted to live and work in County Cavan. It's a great place to be a restaurateur and chef, so many thanks to all of those involved in the excellent tourism board and county council.

To all the close family, friends and babysitters – you know who you are – thank you.

Thank you Orán, Lorcan, Emma and Eoin for being my official tasters and never once refusing, especially the cookies!

And lastly, to my wife, Tara, for all the laughs and debate, thank you so very much.

contents

breakfast and brunch

children's favourites

sides, stocks and sauces

introduction

Welcome to my gluten-free kitchen. It has been a pleasure to write this cookbook and I hope that those who cook my recipes will find the pleasure of cooking all over again, something that was taken from me briefly when I was first diagnosed with coeliac disease in 2013.

Growing up on a small farm in Cavan, the batch loaf was a staple and unfortunately medical conditions that were based on dietary intolerances were unheard of around this time. Many households in the county were brought up with this on the table – unluckily for those like me.

As a child I was in and out of hospital with cramps and various others symptoms of coeliac disease. I was always bloated and tired. It wasn't unheard of for me to fall asleep in class, both as a child and as a teenager. For a long time, this condition crippled every aspect of my life.

School was a huge challenge and the symptoms of being a coeliac were interpreted as my lack of interest in education. Participating in activities was difficult, as evening times were particularly hard due to the constant tiredness and lack of energy. I'm glad awareness of coeliac disease is at an all-time high and that I have finally got something good from the condition – this book!

My love and appreciation of cooking and good produce wasn't accidental, and if I'm honest, the 'having to' cook came before the love and appreciation bit. My mother was the main (gluten-filled) breadwinner (excuse the pun!) and consequently I took on a lot of the household duties, including cooking. We rarely bought anything as we had our own small plot of potatoes, cabbage, carrots and rhubarb to pick from outside our back door.

As school was so challenging, the obvious career path for me was something apprentice based. I applied to the Killybegs IT to study Professional Cookery, but I wasn't successful due to the huge demand at that time. Feeling somewhat discouraged, I decided that instead of harbouring pipe dreams about becoming a chef, I would actually lay pipes and so I embarked on a brief stint as an apprentice plumber.

I remember working near Pembroke Road in Dublin and knowing that I needed to follow my dream of being a chef. As fate, luck and the gods would have it, the company that I was working with was equally as unimpressed with my pipe-laying skills as I was, so I was duly let go. That same day I got a call from Killybegs to say that a space had opened up on their Professional Cookery course.

It was there that I started to hone my skills in the kitchen and where I met my wife, Tara. Doors began to open and my first introduction to good food and good produce was from Pat Kerley in Dundalk. From there, I moved on to Thornton's in Dublin along the Portobello canal and spent two years working under Kevin Thornton.

Both Pat Kerley and Kevin Thornton have an immense love of good ingredients and use only the best produce. My time with them had a huge influence on my approach to cooking. Olivier Meisonnave, who worked with Kevin before opening his own restaurant, Dax, gave me an insight into what it takes to run a seamless front of house. I worked in Le Coq Hardi with John Howard in its final year and he instilled the art of food and business in me.

In 2001, I won the Euro-toques Young Chef of the Year award and also spent a couple months in New York. Tara and I came back to Cavan, where I opened my first restaurant, The Oak Room, in 2001 before we moved to The Olde Post Inn in 2002. Our core team is made up of Garret Galligan, who has been with us since the beginning, and Brid Teevan, our pastry chef who joined us in 2007. They both have a real understanding of our philosophy and what is important to us: quality, seasonality and local ingredients where possible. We've built an excellent rapport with the local producers in our area and most of the ingredients we use in the restaurant come from the surrounding counties.

My wife pushed me towards the diagnosis when the symptoms of the condition became unbearable. After so many years, I had come to accept that feeling lethargic, bloated and suffering from daily stomach cramps and other unpleasant symptoms was normal. But there came a point when I could no longer blame the long working hours for my lack of energy or the feeling of being bloated on overindulging in the kitchen.

The diagnosis was a revelation. Not knowing what was wrong had been as intolerable as my intolerance to gluten. Having lived with constant sickness since childhood, the relief that came a few weeks after eliminating gluten from my diet was immense. But when I was finally diagnosed, I couldn't get my head around it at first. I remember pulling into a supermarket afterwards and there was absolutely nothing I could eat – the sandwich before heading into the restaurant for the night was gone. There was only one option, and that was to get myself organised. And so the challenge began.

I devoured reading material on the condition and started to pay more attention to food labels, but the initial adjustment period wasn't easy. But when I started to feel well, it gave me a new lease on life and I knew it was time to start getting the meals I missed and loved back into my life. I've even started to see the silver lining on the grey cloud, as my diet and that of my family is much healthier and more balanced. Tara and I have four children and we all eat the same meals. Of course, sometimes a batch loaf does make an appearance!

Since being diagnosed with coeliac disease, there has not been one day that I have felt unwell. That said, if you enjoy good food and dining out, as I do, encountering a blasé attitude about the condition is commonplace and I have inevitably fallen foul of an accidental gluten overdose that conjures up bad memories.

This book isn't another book detailing the ins and outs or ups and downs of coeliac disease – very simply, it's a cookbook. The recipes just so happen to not include gluten. Recreating dishes over the years such as Yorkshire puddings, fish and chips, pasta and pastries was a trial and error experiment that we all enjoyed at The Olde Post Inn. We take great pride knowing that coeliac or not, all our customers are guaranteed a dining experience to remember. Writing this book has been an enjoyable experience that has allowed us to compile all our recipes for others to enjoy.

I frequently hear it said that a coeliac will know that food contains gluten or wheat because it will taste too good not to. I hope that this book is filled with recipes that will dispel that myth and that everybody will enjoy and delight in the recipes, whether or not you're a coeliac.

a brief explanation of coeliac disease

In case you are using this book to cook for a friend or family member who has coeliac disease, or if you are newly diagnosed, I thought a brief overview of what it means to be coeliac might be helpful.

According to the HSE, coeliac disease is a common digestive condition where a person is intolerant (has an adverse reaction) to the protein gluten. If someone with coeliac disease is exposed to gluten, they may experience a wide range of symptoms and adverse effects, including:

- diarrhoea
- bloating
- abdominal pain
- weight loss
- failure to grow at the expected rate
- malnutrition

Coeliac disease is an auto-immune disease, which means that the body's immune system attacks itself. When people with this condition eat gluten, this results in damage to the lining of the small intestine, which stops the body properly absorbing nutrients. The symptoms of coeliac disease can range from very mild to severe.

Gluten is a protein that is found in the following cereals:
- wheat
- barley
- rye
- oats (only gluten-free pure oats are suitable for coeliacs and then only after the first year and with monitoring by health professionals, as up to 5% of coeliacs may not be able to tolerate even pure oats)

During the 1980s, before advances in testing for coeliac disease were made, the condition was mistakenly thought to be rare.

However, coeliac disease is now known to be a common condition that affects approximately 1 in every 100 people. Women are two to three times more likely to develop coeliac disease than men. Cases of coeliac disease have been diagnosed in people of all ages.

In some cases, coeliac disease does not cause any noticeable symptoms, or it causes very mild symptoms. As a result, it is thought that at least 50% or possibly as many as 90% of cases are either undiagnosed or misdiagnosed as other digestive conditions, such as irritable bowel syndrome (IBS).

The cause or causes of coeliac disease are unknown, but it is thought to be associated with a combination of genetic and environmental factors. (www.hse.ie/eng/health/az/C/Coeliac-disease)

tips and essentials

The biggest obstacle I had to overcome when I was diagnosed was the mental block of how to manoeuvre around gluten in my cooking. The relief of understanding why I was constantly fatigued and bloated was overshadowed by how difficult it seemed to continue cooking good food. I even had to keep an eye on whether the protein is hidden in any oral care products, such as toothpaste, and I quickly learned to check the labels of simple pleasures such as bars of chocolate.

It took time to filter information from trusted sources and learn some simple and practical steps, such as 'gluten-proofing' the kitchen by purchasing a new toaster and designating separate cupboards for gluten-free foods. I now follow a few simple rules at home and at work to avoid any cross-contamination of foods:

- I store gluten-free foods in a separate cupboard in the kitchen.
- I have a separate compartment in the fridge and freezer for gluten-free foods.
- I label and date all foods, especially frozen foods.
- I wash everything well, i.e. kitchen surfaces, utensils and pans.
- I keep a 'gluten-free' pastry brush, rolling pin and sieve.

A little bit of thought and preparation with your kitchen store cupboard goes a long way towards preparing any meal at any time of the day. All supermarkets now have a 'free from' section, which makes it easier to narrow down the selection.

One thing that I have found very helpful is planning ahead, making a little more at meal times and freezing where possible. The same rules apply to refrigerating and freezing gluten-free products as to those that contain gluten:

- Set aside a compartment in the freezer for gluten-free items only. Always label and date each item.
- Items like breaded chicken dishes freeze well once layered with parchment paper in an airtight container. When needed, take them out of the freezer the night before and defrost in the refrigerator rather than the microwave.
- I freeze my bread already sliced and portioned and take it out as I need it. There is less waste this way.
- Make breadcrumbs with your leftover gluten-free bread and freeze for later use.
- You can freeze your homemade stocks in airtight containers with tight-fitting lids. Be sure to allow room in the container for expansion.
- Try not to keep anything in the freezer for more than four weeks, as chances are you won't use it after this time and it will deteriorate in quality.

Foods to avoid

As a coeliac, being mindful of what you can and can't buy in a supermarket is important. Thankfully, food labelling is now much clearer, with allergens listed in bold print, although coeliacs still have to be aware of the possibility of cross-contamination where a product has been manufactured. When you're shopping, always double check labels and look in particular at the ingredient listing of processed foods.

In general you should avoid the following unless the ingredient/product specifically says it is gluten free:

- Flours or grains of wheat, rye and barley, including spelt flour
- Oats, unless specifically stated as being gluten-free
- Batter, breadcrumbs and pastry
- Pasta, couscous and bulgur wheat
- Marinades, sauces, mayonnaise, pickles and gravy mixes
- Soya sauce
- Stock or bouillon
- Modified starch
- Malt or malt flavouring (a common ingredient in breakfast cereals)
- Any ingredient listed as a 'natural flavouring'
- Processed meat or seafood, especially finished with any sauces or stuffings
- Beer, ale, lager and stout

The Coeliac Society of Ireland produces an annual food list to help you choose suitable gluten-free products (www.coeliac-ireland.com). There is a large list of forbidden ingredients, such as malt extract, which are usually found in processed and prepared foods. In general, it's best to avoid processed and prepared foods unless they are specifically marked as gluten-free.

Naturally gluten-free foods

Many foods are naturally gluten-free, such as fruit, vegetables, nuts, seeds, pulses, meat, poultry, fish, eggs, soya, milk, cheese, natural yoghurt, cream, rice, corn (maize), tapioca, polenta, buckwheat, sago, arrowroot, cornflour, millet flour, gram flour (chickpea flour), potato flour, soya flour, chestnut flour, teff, quinoa and fresh yeasts (check yeast extracts), as well as sugar, honey, golden syrup, maple syrup, treacle, jams and marmalades, natural vanilla extract, butter, margarine and cooking oils.

Gluten-free flour

In order to get a good end result, you will need a blend of various different flours. No one gluten-free flour works entirely on its own, so you can choose to create your own flour blends at home (which can be quite a hassle) or use the ready-blended varieties that are now widely available in supermarkets.

With gluten-free baking in particular, it has taken me a lot of trial and error to overcome the short, grainy texture that you can get in a lot of gluten-free products. By testing the various gluten-free brands on offer, I have found the following give the best results.

- Doves Farm white bread flour blend (contains rice, potato, tapioca and xanthan gum)
- Doves Farm plain white flour blend (contains rice, potato, tapioca, maize and buckwheat)
- Doves Farm white self-raising flour blend (contains, rice, potato, tapioca, maize,

buckwheat and raising agents, monocalcium, phosphate, sodium bicarbonate and xanthan gum)

- Odlums gluten-free/tritamyl flour (contains maize starch, milk powder, rice flour, soya bran, raising agents, fruit fibre, soya flour, salt, calcium carbonate, preservative, stabiliser, vitamins B1 and B2, niacin and iron)

Baking aids
Gums
One of the essential ingredients in gluten-free baking is xanthan gum. It acts like gluten in flour and gives your product stretch and elasticity. It also helps to bind ingredients, making your product less brittle. A flour blend may already contain a gum, but you will still need to add more in some recipes. Xanthan gum is a powder and can be sourced in most supermarkets or health food shops.

Baking powder
Standard baking powder often contains gluten. Gluten-free baking powder is now widely available in the baking section of supermarkets. Bread soda (bicarbonate of soda) and cream of tartar are naturally gluten-free, so if you prefer to make your own gluten-free baking powder, simply mix two parts bicarbonate of soda with one part cream of tartar and use this in place of regular baking powder, spoon for spoon.

Cornflour, potato flour or arrowroot
If you wish to thicken sauces, any of these will work.

Cereals
There are numerous shop-bought gluten-free cereals, such as gluten-free cornflakes, which are quick and handy.

Gluten-free porridge oats
Gluten-free porridge oats are ideal for using in any baking recipe and are delicious for breakfast, especially in the cereal bars on page 6. When using oats, it is important that you use a gluten-free variety, as oat crops can be cross-contaminated with other crops, such as wheat. Avenin, a protein found in oats, is similar to gluten and should be avoided if you are sensitive to it. However, research has shown that most people with coeliac disease can safely eat avenin (www.coeliac.org.uk/gluten-free-diet-and-lifestyle/gf-diet/oats).

Gluten-free pasta, noodles and rice
Gluten-free pasta is becoming more common and is readily available in most supermarkets. Most of the gluten-free pastas available are rice or corn based. The one thing to be careful of when cooking gluten-free pasta is that there is no room for error, unlike conventional pasta. Once the pasta is just cooked, remove it from the heat, drain and serve. Rice noodles are gluten-free.

Rice is absolutely essential for your store cupboard. While many people think of rice as a simple side dish, it's excellent when cooked as a meal in its own right and it readily absorbs other flavours from stocks and spices. It's also incredibly quick and easy to prepare.

Rice is a grain of cultivated grasses and is one of the world's staple foods. The different cultivation techniques, as well as cross-breeding, have resulted in thousands of varieties of rice, including sticky rice, wild rice and fragrant rice. Rice can be categorised as long, medium or short grain. Long-grain rice, such as basmati, is thin, dainty and pointed. Medium-grain and short-grain rice are plumper, starchier and more absorbent. Examples of medium-grain rice are risotto rice, such as Arborio, while examples of short-grain rice include pudding rice and sushi rice.

Other grains

Buckwheat is the seed of the buckwheat plant, which can be used as a grain or ground into flour. Unlike other cereals, buckwheat doesn't contain gluten. It comes roasted or raw and you can sprout it if you buy it in the raw state. Buckwheat has a full, nutty flavour.

Millet is frequently used in Africa and Asia as an important source of dietary fibre and iron. Millet is sadly overlooked in the West, where it is most often encountered as animal fodder. There are many varieties of millet, found primarily in the form of grains, flakes and flour.

Polenta is a granular form of maize meal and has become a staple in Italian cooking. It can be served hot or cold, and once cooked it's highly versatile. It's also a great alternative to breadcrumbs.

Quinoa is a useful addition to the diet, as it is a good source of protein as well as being gluten-free.

It's a great substitute for couscous or bulgur wheat in salads and side dishes.

Pulses and beans

Pulses and beans can be used in stews and casseroles, but are also great in salads or as side dishes in their own right. Choose from fresh, tinned or dried, depending on your preference and availability.

Black beans have a rich flavour and velvety texture and they hold their shape well during cooking. Black beans are a particularly good source of antioxidants, iron and protein. They are a staple of South American cooking and are particularly delicious in soups and stews.

Black-eyed beans are small, creamy-flavoured beans with a black mark where they were joined to the pod. They are much used in American and African cooking.

Borlotti beans are a variety of kidney bean with a nutty flavour. Italy's noble bean grows in cream and claret flecked pods and are available fresh when in season, or dried or tinned all year round. They are especially good when cooked with aromatic herbs like rosemary, sage or basil and work well when added to sauces or a risotto. They can be substituted for red or white beans in many recipes.

Fresh broad beans are sweet and delicious pod beans with a smooth, creamy texture. They only have a short season during the summer, so they are often dried, canned or frozen to preserve them. Fresh beans are more popular than the dried variety, which tend to be quite floury. Young, thin beans are eaten pods and all, but larger, older broad beans need to have the tough pods removed.

Butter beans (also called lima beans or marrow beans) are large, creamy-coloured beans that have a soft, floury texture when cooked. They do well in mixed bean salads or rich, wintry stews. They are also a useful source of potassium.

Cannellini beans are small, white, kidney-shaped beans that are good for using in salads and casseroles.

Chickpeas are a small legume that is popular in Mediterranean, Middle Eastern and Indian cooking. Chickpeas originated in Asia and travelled to the Mediterranean. They are therefore a humble staple of many cultures and are highly versatile. Use them in salads, soups, casseroles and in the famous Middle Eastern dishes of hummus and falafel. They can also be ground into gram flour, which is widely used in Indian and Bangladeshi cuisine to make pastries and bhajis.

Flageolet beans are small, creamy, pale green beans with tender skin and a fine, delicate flavour, and are much prized in France. They are actually small, young haricot beans that have been harvested and dried before they are fully ripe. Use them in tomato-based stews, in mixed bean salads or tossed in olive oil to accompany rich main courses.

Haricot beans are small, oval, plump and creamy white with a mild flavour and a smooth, buttery texture. Haricot beans are widely used in the cooking of countries such as France, Spain, Portugal and South America. With little flavour of their own, they absorb other aromas and flavours easily, which makes them popular in slow-cooked dishes such as cassoulet or bean purées.

Kidney beans are reddish-brown kidney-shaped pulses with a soft, creamy flesh. Dried kidney beans need soaking and should be cooked carefully because they contain toxins on the outer skin when raw, which are rendered harmless by boiling. They're great in mixed bean salads and stews such as chilli con carne.

Lentils are a large family of pulses with many varieties, sizes and colours. Most lentils don't need soaking before cooking. Some hold their shape well when cooked whereas others collapse, so you need to decide what kind of recipe you are using the lentils for and choose accordingly. Whole lentils are good in hot or cold salads as well as accompaniments for rich main dishes, or they can be added to soups and stews.

Seeds

Linseed or flaxseed is a good source of the essential fatty acid omega-3.

Pumpkin seeds are featured in the recipes of many cultures and are a special hallmark of traditional Mexican cuisine. Pumpkin seeds have recently become more popular as research suggests that they have unique nutritional and health benefits. They are a good source of protein and minerals, including iron, zinc and phosphorus.

Sesame seeds are probably the oldest crop grown for its taste, dating back 2,000 years to China. Sesame was imported from India to Europe during the first century. Persians used sesame oil because they had no olive oil. A good source of protein, sesame seeds also contain calcium, iron and magnesium.

Sunflower seeds are native to South America. Sunflower is an important crop in many parts of Europe, chiefly for the light cooking oil that is extracted from its seeds. High in polyunsaturated and monounsaturated fats, sunflower oil is widely used in frying and as a salad oil. In many Mediterranean countries, roasted and salted sunflower seeds in their shells are a popular snack. Sunflower seeds can also be sprouted and added to salads, being highly nutritious and pleasantly nutty. They are also good for protein.

Sauces/miscellaneous

Mustard powder is made by grinding brown and white mustard seeds. You simply mix it with equal amounts of water to create a pungent condiment to add to dressings, sauces and sandwiches. Please note that some ready-made versions of this product contain wheat flour.

Gluten-free versions of soya sauce, Worcestershire sauce and bouillon and stock cubes are also available and are handy store cupboard staples.

Notes for all recipes

- The recipe measurements are as accurate as possible, but there may be variation depending on what products you buy.
- Level spoon measures are used throughout.
- Large eggs are used throughout.
- Metric measurements are used in the recipes, but there are conversion tables on page 223.

breakfast
and brunch

WHEN I WAS diagnosed as having a gluten intolerance, I was immediately concerned about what I would do without toast in the mornings. My approach to having breakfast needed to change, but in a way that was quick, convenient and most importantly, tasty.

Breakfast is the most important meal of the day, so you have to be prepared and have ingredients to hand or give it some thought the night before. This chapter contains some tried and tested breakfast favourites but also some options that are off the beaten track.

smoothies

SERVES 4 • MIXED BERRY SMOOTHIE

250g frozen mixed berries

250g low-fat natural yoghurt

250ml freshly squeezed orange juice

2 tsp honey

**BANANA, MANGO
AND BLUEBERRY SMOOTHIE**

1 banana

1 ripe mango, peeled and stone removed

150g frozen blueberries

100g low-fat natural yoghurt

100g coconut cream

250ml freshly squeezed orange juice

2 tsp honey

**BEETROOT AND
STRAWBERRY SMOOTHIE**

250g low-fat natural yoghurt

150g cooked beetroot

125g frozen strawberries

200ml freshly squeezed orange juice

2 tsp hemp seeds

2 tsp honey

If you're trying to introduce more variety into your diet or those in your household, smoothies are a great way of disguising some vegetables or fruits that you struggle to eat. In adding hemp seeds to any smoothie, you are increasing its nutritive value. This is particularly important as a gluten-free diet can be lacking in minerals, vitamins and fibre, and it also helps to increase fibre in children's diet.

Place all the ingredients in a blender or food processor and blend until smooth. Serve immediately in a large glass.

GET AHEAD

Covered well, these smoothies will keep for up to two days in the fridge – just give them a good stir before serving.

buttermilk scones

MAKES 10 SCONES

150g gluten-free self-raising flour

150g gluten-free white flour blend, plus extra for dusting

1 tsp gluten-free baking powder

½ tsp xanthan gum

½ tsp bread soda

½ tsp salt

40g caster sugar, plus extra for dusting

70g butter, cubed

50g dried fruit, such as sultanas, raisins or cranberries (optional)

1 egg

200ml buttermilk approximately

jam, to serve (optional)

whipped cream, to serve (optional)

These light scones are ideal for a mid-morning snack. They are delicious freshly baked and served with jam.

Preheat the oven to 200°C. Dust a large non-stick baking tray (30cm x 23cm x 5cm) with a little flour.

Sieve the flours, baking powder, xanthan gum, bread soda and salt into a large bowl. Add the sugar and mix together. Rub in the butter with your fingertips until it's a sandy texture, then stir in the dried fruit, if using, and make a well in the centre.

Whisk the egg, but reserve a tablespoon of it for later. Add the beaten egg and 150ml of the buttermilk to the flour and mix until it's all incorporated. If the dough isn't bound together, add the rest of the buttermilk, little by little, until you achieve the required consistency, which should be soft to the touch. Gentle handling is essential to produce a light scone.

Transfer the dough onto a lightly floured board and pat down until it's 3cm thick. Use a 4cm scone cutter to stamp out the scones.

Place on the prepared baking tray, then brush the scones with the remaining egg and sprinkle with a little caster sugar or flour. Put the scones in the oven, then immediately reduce the temperature to 180°C and bake for 20–25 minutes, until they are well risen, golden brown and firm. Transfer to a wire rack and leave to cool.

To serve, slice the scones, spread with jam and top with whipped cream.

GET AHEAD

Once baked, the scones can be wrapped individually and frozen.

breakfast cereal bars

MAKES 16 BARS

1 x 397g tin of condensed milk

½ tbsp honey

200g gluten-free rolled oats

125g chopped nuts, such as Brazil nuts, hazelnuts, pistachios and pecans

120g mixed seeds, such as pumpkin, sunflower and sesame

100g mixed dried fruit, such as figs, cranberries, cherries, pineapple, apricot and blueberries, roughly chopped

75g desiccated coconut

2 dessertspoons hemp seeds (optional)

Initially I thought that cereal bars were difficult and time consuming to make, but we have discovered quite the opposite. In fact, they can be fun for all the family to make. It's also a great way to encourage younger children to try different varieties of nuts, seeds and fruit.

Preheat the oven to 130°C. Line a baking tin (ideally one that is 23cm square and 3.5cm deep) with non-stick baking paper.

Warm the condensed milk in the microwave for approximately 2 minutes. You can also do this on the hob, but it can be prone to burning if you don't keep an eye on it. Add the honey to the milk and stir.

Mix all the dry ingredients in a large bowl. Add the milk and honey to the dry ingredients and mix well with a spatula. Spread the mixture into the prepared baking tin and bake in the oven for 50 minutes, until a light golden colour. Take out and allow to cool completely in the tin. Once cooled, cut into approx. 16 squares. The bars should be firm yet a little chewy. These cereal bars can be stored up to a week in a sealed container.

granola

MAKES 10 SERVINGS

100ml maple syrup

2 tbsp vegetable oil

2 tsp honey

1 tsp vanilla essence

225g gluten-free oats

60g flaked almonds

40g sunflower seeds

40g pumpkin seeds

4 tsp sesame seeds

100g dried cranberries

40g coconut flakes

Granola is a bit of a treat at breakfast time and is a great addition to natural yoghurt and any fresh fruit, or eaten simply with milk. I make my own as there is a lot of processed sugar in the commercial packets.

Preheat the oven to 160°C.

Mix the maple syrup, oil, honey and vanilla essence in a large bowl. Add the oats, almonds and seeds and mix well. Pour onto a baking tray and pat out evenly.

Bake for 15 minutes, then remove from the oven and add the dried fruit and coconut to the tray. Return to the oven and cook for a further 15 minutes, until golden. Leave to cool on the tray.

Once completely cooled, remove the granola from the tray and place in an airtight container. This granola should keep for several weeks stored in an airtight container.

soda bread

MAKES 1 LOAF

450g gluten-free white bread flour blend, plus extra for dusting

1 tsp bread soda

1 tsp salt

1 tbsp caster sugar

430ml buttermilk

This is a very crusty, light bread. Like all good homemade soda bread, it needs to be consumed within 24 hours.

Preheat the oven to 200°C. Dust a baking tray with a little flour.

Sieve the flour, bread soda and salt into a large bowl, then add the caster sugar and mix together. Make a well in the centre of the flour mix and add the buttermilk.

Using one hand in a claw shape, gently mix everything together, working from the sides of the bowl. The dough should be soft and wet but not too sticky. Once it comes together, pour it out onto a well-floured worktop.

With floured hands, shape the dough into a round without overworking the dough. Place the round loaf on the baking tray, cut a deep cross across the top and bake for 25 minutes. Remove the loaf from the oven, turn it over and put it back on the tray and continue to bake for an additional 10 minutes. The bread is done when it sounds hollow when you tap the bottom. Leave to cool on a wire rack.

bread rolls

MAKES 8–10 ROLLS

500g gluten-free white bread flour blend, plus extra for dusting

60g butter, softened

1 tsp xanthan gum

1 tsp salt

20g fresh yeast or 1½ tsp fast action dried yeast

1 tbsp caster sugar

1 egg

200ml lukewarm water

1 dessertspoon milk

selection of seeds, such as linseeds, sesame (white and black), poppy, sunflower and pumpkin

FOR THE EGG WASH:

1 egg yolk

1 dessertspoon milk

These rolls are suitable for serving at any time of the day and make a wonderful centrepiece on the table.

Place the flour, butter, xanthan gum and salt into the bowl of a stand mixer. If using dried yeast, add it at this point too. Use the dough hook attachment to combine all the ingredients.

Combine the sugar, egg, water, milk and fresh yeast (if using) in a large jug and mix well. Add to the dry ingredients and mix with the dough hook for 8–10 minutes. Leave the dough in the bowl, cover it with cling film and put in a warm place for at least 1 hour. It will increase in size.

Dust the worktop with some flour and transfer the dough onto the worktop. Cut into 8–10 equal portions and shape into rounds. If the dough is too sticky when you are forming the rolls, rub some olive oil on your hands. This will prevent the dough from sticking to your hands. Place the rolls in a 22cm round tin. Mix the egg yolk and milk together and brush the tops of the rolls with the egg wash. Sprinkle with the seeds and leave in a warm place to prove for 40 minutes, uncovered. The dough will rise again.

Meanwhile, preheat the oven to 200°C.

Bake the rolls for 20 minutes, until crusty on top. Turn the rolls over in the tin to allow the base to get crusty too. To check that the rolls are done, turn them over and tap the base. If you hear a light, hollow sound, the rolls are ready for serving.

eggs benedict

SERVES 4

200ml hollandaise (page 151)

8 slices of rindless streaky bacon

30ml white wine vinegar

salt and freshly ground black pepper

4 eggs

2 gluten-free bagels, cut in half

Chopped fresh chives, to garnish

This is a great Saturday morning breakfast or brunch. It's worth the effort to make the hollandaise, as it's such a filling dish that you can skip lunch. Alternatively, you can substitute spinach for the bacon and have eggs Florentine.

First make the hollandaise sauce according to the instructions on page 151.

Grill the streaky bacon until crisp, then set aside on a plate lined with kitchen paper to absorb any excess grease.

To poach the eggs, fill a medium-sized pot with 1 litre of water, then add the vinegar and a pinch of salt. Bring to the boil, then reduce to a simmer – the water should be lightly bubbling under the surface. Stir the water with a spoon, as this will help the egg white to completely encase the egg yolk and the end result will be a perfectly shaped poached egg. Break the egg into the centre of the pot while the water is swirling round. Repeat the process with each egg. The eggs should take approximately 4 minutes to cook. The egg white should be slightly firm and the yolk should still be runny. Remove from the water with a slotted spoon and set aside to drain on kitchen paper.

Toast each bagel half, then place on a baking tray. Place two slices of bacon on each bagel half, then place a poached egg on each, followed by a dessertspoon of hollandaise on top.

Place the baking tray under a hot grill to gently warm the hollandaise and give it a light brown colour. Serve immediately on warmed plates and garnish with chopped chives.

savoury egg bakes

MAKES 12

12 slices of Parma ham

1 dessertspoon olive oil, plus extra for greasing

½ red pepper, diced

1 shallot, finely chopped

8 asparagus spears

6 eggs

60g Parmesan cheese, grated

60ml milk

freshly ground black pepper

These are a quick and delicious breakfast that can be made in advance and reheated as required.

Preheat the oven to 180°C. Lightly grease a 12-hole muffin or bun tin.

Line each cup with a slice of Parma ham, covering the base and the sides. Place in the oven for 5 minutes, until semi-cooked, then remove from the oven and set aside. Heat the oil in a small frying pan and cook the red pepper and shallot for 4 minutes, until soft. Remove from the heat and set aside to cool.

To prepare the asparagus, snap the tough ends off the spears (approx. 4–5cm off the ends), then carefully peel the ends of the stalk without removing too much actual asparagus. Add them to a small saucepan of lightly boiling water and cook for approximately 2 minutes, until they are tender but still have a bit of bite. Remove the spears from the water and plunge into a bowl of ice-cold water to stop them from cooking further. Drain and cut into bite-sized pieces.

In a mixing bowl, beat the eggs with a fork, then add the cooked asparagus, red pepper and shallot along with the Parmesan and milk. Season with pepper (you shouldn't need any extra salt, as the Parma ham is already salty).

Pour a ladleful of the egg mixture into each of the Parma ham cases and return to the oven to cook for 12 minutes, until set but soft in the centre and golden.

GET AHEAD

The egg bakes can be kept fresh for two or three days well covered in the fridge or you can wrap them individually and freeze for up to four weeks.

ham, cherry tomato, mushroom and cheddar omelette

SERVES 2

2 tsp olive oil

1 large Portobello mushroom, sliced

4 eggs, beaten

salt and freshly ground black pepper

5 cherry tomatoes, roughly chopped

30g cooked ham, cut into pieces

30g white Cheddar cheese, grated

homemade tomato ketchup (page 154), to serve

Eggs are the most versatile ingredient in the kitchen, and are incredibly quick and easy to cook. Omelettes are great for using up leftovers or just left plain. When cooking omelettes, try not to overcook the eggs or they will become rubbery and tasteless.

Heat a 25cm non-stick frying pan over a high heat, then drizzle 1 teaspoon of the olive oil onto the pan. Sauté the mushroom in the pan for 1 minute, until tender, then remove from the pan and set aside.

Add the remaining teaspoon of olive oil to the pan over a medium heat. Beat the eggs in a bowl and lightly season with salt and pepper, then add to the pan, swirling the egg with the fork. When the egg is partially cooked – it should still have a runny consistency but is starting to set – sprinkle the cooked mushrooms, tomatoes, ham and cheese on top of the omelette, then fold the omelette in half and cook for a further minute, until light golden but still with a slightly runny consistency in the centre.

Slide the omelette onto a chopping board and cut in half. Serve on preheated plates with homemade tomato ketchup and season to taste.

pork, jalapeño pepper, coriander, lime and egg bake

SERVES 4

50g butter, melted

200g cooked pork trimmings or bacon pieces

40g gluten-free bread, roughly chopped

20g fresh coriander, chopped

1 red pepper, chopped

1 jalapeño pepper, deseeded and finely chopped

zest and juice of 1 lime

salt and freshly ground black pepper

4 eggs

You can vary the ingredients in this dish to use up any leftovers. It's a lovely breakfast and brunch dish that's perfect after a night out.

Preheat the oven to 200°C. Lightly grease four individual ovenproof dishes approx. 10cm in diameter and 3cm high with some of the melted butter.

Put the rest of the melted butter in a large bowl with the pork, bread, coriander, red pepper, jalapeño pepper and the lime zest and juice. Lightly season with salt and pepper and mix together, then divide evenly between the four dishes.

Place the dishes on a baking tray and bake in the oven for 8 minutes, until golden. Remove the tray from the oven and reduce the temperature to 175°C.

Break an egg into the centre of each dish. Return to the oven for a further 7 minutes, until the egg white is almost cooked. The egg yolk should still be very runny and undercooked. It will act like a sauce for the dish when mixed with the other hot ingredients, which will cook it further. Carefully remove from the oven and serve straight away.

ham and cheese crêpes

MAKES 8 CRÊPES

250g gluten-free plain white flour blend

¼ tsp salt

2 eggs, beaten

600ml milk

100ml water

80g butter, melted

200g cooked ham or cooked bacon, chopped

200g Cheddar cheese, grated

20ml olive oil

freshly ground black pepper

tomato relish, to serve

These savoury crêpes are very versatile and any combination of fillings will work. Try bacon and a little crème fraîche, spinach and mushrooms or whatever leftovers you may have.

Preheat the oven to 165°C. Line a baking tray with non-stick baking paper.

Sieve the flour and salt into a large bowl. Make a well in the centre and add the eggs, then pour in the milk and water. Mix with a hand-held mixer, whisk or in a food processor until a smooth batter is achieved with no lumps. Add 1 tablespoon of the melted butter to the batter and mix it through fully. Set the batter aside while you prepare the filling.

Heat a crêpe pan or non-stick pan over a medium heat. Add a drizzle of the melted butter to the pan, then add a small amount of batter – you just want a thin layer covering the base of the pan. Cook the crêpes on each side until they are light golden. A spatula is handy for turning the crêpes.

Slide the crêpe out of the pan. Scatter some ham and cheese down the centre of each crêpe, drizzle with a little olive oil, season with freshly ground black pepper, roll up and set aside. Repeat the process for the remaining crêpes, adding a drizzle of melted butter to the pan each time.

Once all the crêpes are prepared, place them on the lined tray and bake in the oven for 3 minutes, until the filling is warmed through and the cheese is starting to melt. Serve at once with tomato relish.

sweet crêpes

MAKES 8 CRÊPES

250g gluten-free plain white flour blend

25g caster sugar

¼ tsp salt

3 eggs

500ml milk

100ml water

50g butter, melted

TO SERVE (OPTIONAL):

2 tsp caster sugar

1 lemon, cut in half

maple syrup

This is a real family favourite in my house. The batter only takes minutes to prepare or it can even be made the night before. The beauty of using gluten-free flour for crêpes is that the batter doesn't need much time to rest before cooking.

Sieve the flour, sugar and salt into a large bowl. Make a well in the centre and add the eggs, then pour in the milk and water. Mix with a hand-held mixer, whisk or in a food processor until a smooth batter is achieved with no lumps. Add 1 dessertspoon of the melted butter to the batter and mix it through fully.

Heat a crêpe pan or non-stick pan over a medium heat. Add a drizzle of the melted butter to the pan, then add a small amount of batter – you just want a thin layer covering the base of the pan. Cook the crêpes on each side until they are light golden. A spatula is handy for turning the crêpes. Once cooked, turn out onto a warm plate. Repeat the process for the remaining crêpes, adding a drizzle of melted butter to the pan each time.

To serve, sprinkle with a little caster sugar and a squeeze of lemon, or alternatively drizzle with a little maple syrup.

GET AHEAD

The crêpes can be kept warm by sitting a plate over a small saucepan of simmering water and placing parchment paper between each crêpe to stop them sticking together.

red pepper and bacon hash browns

SERVES 4–6

165g streaky bacon

400g potatoes, peeled and grated

salt and freshly ground black pepper

50g butter

½ red pepper, finely diced

1 shallot, finely diced

4–6 eggs, to serve

2–3 tbsp vegetable oil (if frying the eggs)

30ml white wine vinegar (if poaching the eggs)

This is quite a filling and substantial breakfast. You can change the mixture to include mushrooms, fresh herbs, chilli, courgette or whatever leftovers you need to use up.

Preheat the oven to 180°C. Grill the streaky bacon until crisp, then roughly chop and set aside on a plate lined with kitchen paper to absorb any excess grease. Once the potatoes have been peeled and grated, place them into a clean tea towel and twist to squeeze out the excess moisture. Put the prepared potato into a large bowl and lightly season with salt and pepper.

Place a small frying pan over a medium heat. Add a knob of butter along with the red pepper and shallot and cook for about 3 minutes, until soft. Add the chopped bacon, red pepper and shallot to the grated potatoes and mix together.

Heat a large non-stick frying pan over a medium heat. Add half of the remaining butter, then add the potato mixture, pressing it down in an even layer. Cook for 5 minutes, then turn the potato mixture over, add the remaining butter and cook for a further 5 minutes, until golden brown. Slide onto a baking tray and bake in the oven for 10 minutes, until crispy.

Meanwhile, if you want to fry the eggs, heat the vegetable oil in a non-stick pan set over a medium heat, then crack an egg into the frying pan of warm oil. Cook until the white is set and the yolk has achieved the finish you like: soft, medium or over easy. If you would prefer to poach the eggs, follow the instructions on page 15.

Place the hash browns on a chopping board and cut into four even wedges. Serve with a poached or fried egg.

GET AHEAD

This can be made the night before and reheated in the morning. Portioned and individually wrapped, these hash browns are also suitable for freezing.

welsh rarebit with mushrooms

SERVES 4

450g button mushrooms or wild mushrooms (girolles, morels, oyster)

350g red Cheddar cheese, grated

2 eggs, beaten

2 dessertspoons wholegrain mustard

1 tbsp Tabasco sauce

salt and freshly ground black pepper

4 thick slices of gluten-free bread

4 thick slices of cooked ham

120g butter

sprig of thyme

2 garlic cloves, crushed

juice of ½ lemon

This is incredibly tasty and quite quick to prepare and can be served on its own, as it's quite filling.

Wipe the mushrooms clean, then cut into slices or quarters. Mix the cheese, eggs, mustard, Tabasco and seasoning together in a bowl.

Chargrill or toast the slices of bread, then place a slice of ham on top of each slice of bread. Place on a baking tray, then spoon the cheese mixture evenly on top of the ham. Put the bread back under the grill until the cheese bubbles and browns.

While the toast is under the grill, fry the mushrooms in a frying pan over a high heat with the butter and thyme until soft, then add the garlic and lemon juice and cook for 2–3 minutes. Serve on top of the toast.

GET AHEAD

The cheese mixture and the mushrooms can both be prepared in advance.

black and white pudding terrine

SERVES 10

520g gluten-free white pudding

180g chicken breast

salt and freshly ground black pepper

520g gluten-free black pudding

8 slices of bacon

This terrine is a breakfast favourite when served with poached eggs, or it can be jazzed up and served as a starter in the autumn and winter with an apple purée or the apple and Calvados sauce on page 155. You can find gluten-free black and white pudding in most supermarkets these days.

Preheat the oven to 180°C. Line a 1kg (2lb) loaf tin with layers of cling film, allowing the cling film to fall over the edges of the tin

Break up the white pudding by hand and set aside in a bowl.

Mince the chicken breast in a food processor by blending for 2 minutes. Remove half of the chicken and set it aside. Add the white pudding and some salt and pepper to the chicken in the food processor and mix for a further 2 minutes. Using a spatula, scrape the mixture into a bowl and set aside.

Now break up the black pudding by hand and place it in the food processor with the remaining minced chicken and some salt and pepper. Mix for 2 minutes, until thoroughly combined. Using a spatula, scrape the mixture into a bowl.

Line the tin neatly with the slices of bacon across the width of the tin without overlapping the bacon. Ensure that lengths of the bacon fall over the sides. Using your hands, place an even layer of the black pudding mixture across the bottom of the tin, leaving it half full. Pat down the mixture. Repeat the process with the white pudding. There should be two layers of alternating colours. Bring the bacon layers over the mixture to cover it.

Wrap the tin tightly with five layers of cling film, ensuring it is completely covered and watertight. Place the tin in a roasting tray, then pour in enough water to come about one-quarter of the way up the sides of the loaf tin. Bake in the oven for 45 minutes, then remove from the oven and leave to cool. Unwrap the terrine from the cling film – you will need scissors or a sharp knife.

To serve, cut the terrine into 1cm-thick slices and pan-fry with a little butter on a medium heat for 2 minutes on each side, until golden brown. Serve on a warm plate with a poached egg (see page 15) and grilled tomato or as a starter with an apple purée or the apple and calvados sauce on page 155.

GET AHEAD

This terrine is suitable for freezing, although it's best sliced and wrapped individually before placing in the freezer. Remove from the freezer the night before using and allow to defrost to room temperature.

roast fillet of mackerel

SERVES 4

1 lemon

4 x 180g mackerel fillets, off the bone

2 plum tomatoes, cut into quarters

1 courgette, sliced into 0.5cm-thick circles

50ml olive oil

salt and freshly ground black pepper

This breakfast dish is also a great option for lunchtime. Once you have the ingredients prepared, it's quick and easy to make. The added bonus? It's wonderfully healthy.

Preheat the oven to 200°C. Line a 30cm x 25cm baking tray with tin foil, then top with greaseproof paper, making sure there is enough to cover the base of the tray plus excess on each side to allow you to fold it up and meet again in the centre to close.

Cut the lemon in half. Juice one half and cut the remaining half into wedges for serving.

Put the mackerel fillets on the greaseproof paper and place the prepared vegetables around the mackerel. Drizzle the mackerel, tomatoes and courgette with the lemon juice and olive oil, then season lightly with salt and pepper.

Fold up the greaseproof paper, ensuring all the ingredients are inside the paper, like an envelope. Fold up the tin foil and seal tightly to ensure no steam will escape during cooking.

Bake for 10 minutes, then remove the tray from the oven to check that all the ingredients are cooked through. Be careful when you open the envelope, as the steam that will escape could be quite hot. The mackerel should be white in colour and slightly firm with a little give. The tomatoes and courgettes should have retained their shape while still being cooked all the way through.

To serve, place one fillet on a warmed plate with some of the tomatoes and courgettes. Spoon a little of the cooking liquid over the top of the mackerel and serve with a lemon wedge on the side.

lunch

IT CAN BE overwhelming when you are first diagnosed as a coeliac, as many lunchtime staples such as sandwiches are no longer a runner. With some thought and advance preparation, though, there are so many delicious lunch options available for coeliacs.

savoury pastry

**MAKES ENOUGH PASTRY
TO LINE 1 x 25CM FLAN TIN**

250g gluten-free plain white flour blend

½ tsp xanthan gum

¼ tsp salt

110g cold butter, cubed

40–45ml water

This savoury pastry is easy to work with and is no different from a regular shortcrust pastry.

Sieve the flour, xanthan gum and salt together into a large bowl. Rub in the cold cubed butter using your fingertips until it's like fine breadcrumbs. Make a well in the centre and mix in the water. Hold back a little water at first, as different varieties of gluten-free flour can vary in absorption and you might not need all of it. Gently mix together by hand until it just comes together.

Once the pastry has bound together, wrap it in cling film and refrigerate for 1 hour or overnight, or you can freeze the pastry at this point.

camembert quiche

SERVES 6–8

1 batch of gluten-free savoury pastry (page 32)

1 red pepper

1 yellow pepper

1 red onion, cut in half

1 dessertspoon olive oil

5 medium eggs

300ml milk

225ml cream

pinch of cayenne pepper

pinch of ground turmeric

pinch of black onion seeds (optional)

salt and freshly ground black pepper

1 tsp chopped fresh chives

225g Camembert cheese, sliced

organic salad leaves and cooked beetroot, to serve

red onion marmalade (page 162), to serve

new Irish potato and chive salad, to serve

This quiche is a real winner either as a filling lunch or brunch. It freezes well and is packed with flavour.

Preheat the oven to 200°C.

Grease and flour a 25cm loose-bottomed flan tin. Once the pastry has rested, roll it out on a lightly floured board. Place the pastry into the tin by lifting it up with the rolling pin, ensuring it isn't stretched at any point and is in an even layer the whole way around the tin. Remove excess pastry from the top with a sharp knife or roll the rolling pin across the top of the tin. Leave to rest for 30 minutes in the fridge.

While the pastry is resting, place the whole red and yellow peppers in an ovenproof dish with the halved red onion. Drizzle with the olive oil and roast for 20 minutes, until softened. Remove from the oven and leave to cool, then peel the skin off the peppers and cut the peppers into long strips. Evenly chop the red onion.

Reduce the oven temperature to 175°C. Blind bake the pastry by lining the pastry itself with greaseproof paper and placing dried beans on top in an even layer. Bake for 15 minutes, then remove the paper and beans and set aside until required.

Whisk the eggs in a bowl, then add the milk, cream, cayenne, turmeric, black onion seeds (if using) and some salt and pepper and mix again to combine. Stir in the peppers, onion and chives.

If you like, you could put the flan tin on a baking tray at this point to make it easier to transfer to the oven once you've poured in the egg. Pour the egg mixture into the pastry case to within 1.25cm of the rim of the flan tin, then place the sliced cheese on top. Bake for 35 minutes. The quiche should have a golden finish and the egg filling should be soft but only just set.

Serve warm with organic salad leaves and beetroot, red onion marmalade and a new Irish potato and chive salad.

chicken and asparagus quiche

SERVES 8

1 batch of gluten-free savoury pastry (page 32)

½ lemon (if poaching the chicken)

sprig of tarragon (if poaching the chicken)

1 bay leaf (if poaching the chicken)

salt and freshly ground black pepper

2 chicken breasts

16 asparagus spears

5 medium eggs

300ml milk

225ml cream

150g Brie cheese, sliced

seasonal salad leaves, to serve

The main ingredients in this quiche complement each other very well. It can be eaten warm or cold.

Grease and flour a 25cm loose-bottomed flan tin. Once the pastry has rested, roll it out on a lightly floured board. Place the pastry into the tin by lifting it up with the rolling pin, ensuring it isn't stretched at any point and is in an even layer the whole way around the tin. Remove excess pastry from the top with a sharp knife or roll the rolling pin across the top of the tin. Leave to rest for 30 minutes in the fridge.

Preheat the oven to 175°C. Blind bake the pastry by lining the pastry itself with greaseproof paper and placing dried beans on top in an even layer. Bake for 15 minutes, then remove the paper and beans and set aside until required.

Meanwhile, poach or roast the chicken breasts. If poaching, half-fill a medium-sized pot with water, half a lemon, a sprig of tarragon, a bay leaf and some salt and pepper and bring it to the boil. Add the chicken breasts, reduce the heat to a simmer and cook for 20–25 minutes, until cooked all the way through. Leave to cool, then cut into even slices.

If roasting, then place the chicken breasts on a baking tray, season with salt and pepper and cook in the oven, still set at 175°C, for 35 minutes, until cooked all the way through. Leave to cool, then cut into even slices.

To prepare the asparagus, snap the tough ends off the spears (approx. 4–5cm off the ends), then carefully peel the ends of the stalk without removing too much actual asparagus. Bring a small pot of water to the boil and add the asparagus. Cook for 3 minutes, until the asparagus is tender.

Remove from the water and place in a bowl of iced water to cool it quickly to stop it from cooking further and to help it retain its colour. Once the asparagus is completely cool, remove it from the water and leave to drain on kitchen paper, then cut in half down the centre.

Whisk the eggs in a bowl, then add the milk, cream and seasoning and mix again to combine.

Place the sliced chicken into the pastry case. Add the slices of Brie on top of the chicken, then place the asparagus evenly around the base. If you like, you could put the flan tin on a baking tray at this point to make it easier to transfer to the oven once you've poured in the egg. Pour the egg mixture into the pastry case to within 1.25cm of the rim of the flan tin. Bake for 35 minutes. The quiche should have a golden finish and the egg filling should be soft but only just set. Serve warm or cold with seasonal salad leaves.

wild garlic pesto bread

MAKES 2 LOAVES

400g gluten-free white bread flour blend, plus extra for dusting

1 tsp salt

½ tsp xanthan gum

15g fresh yeast or 1 tsp fast action dried yeast

1 heaped tsp butter, softened, plus extra for greasing

250ml warm water

25ml milk

2 dessertspoons wild garlic pesto (page 166)

1 egg yolk

1 dessertspoon milk

selection of seeds, such as linseeds, sesame (white and black), poppy, sunflower and pumpkin

This bread is very versatile, but it's particularly good served like a bruchetta or simply with a soup.

Sieve the flour, salt and xanthan gum into the bowl of a stand mixer. If using dried yeast, add it at this point too. Add the softened butter and use the dough hook attachment to combine all the ingredients.

Combine the warm water and 25ml of milk in a jug, then add the fresh yeast (if using) and allow it to dissolve. Add to the dry ingredients along with the wild garlic pesto and mix with the dough hook for 8–10 minutes. Leave the dough in the mixing bowl, cover it with cling film and put in a warm place for at least 1 hour. It will increase in size.

Dust the worktop with some flour and transfer the dough onto the worktop. Divide in half, shape into a loaf and place each loaf into a greased 1lb loaf tin. If the dough is too sticky when you are forming the loaves, rub some olive oil on your hands. This will prevent the dough from sticking to your hands. Mix the egg yolk and dessertspoon of milk together in a small bowl, then brush the dough evenly with this egg wash. Sprinkle with the seeds and leave the loaves in a warm place to prove for at least 45 minutes. The dough will rise again.

Meanwhile, preheat the oven to 200°C.

Bake the loaves for 20 minutes. Remove the loaves from the tins, place them directly on the oven rack and bake for a further 10 minutes to allow a nice crust to develop. To check that the loaves are done, turn them over and tap the base. If you hear a light, hollow sound, they are ready for serving.

GET AHEAD

When wild garlic is in season, this bread can be made in batches and frozen.

prawns in tempura

SERVES 4

2 litres sunflower oil, for deep frying

20 Dublin Bay prawns or any large fresh prawns

10g fresh coriander, chopped

zest and juice of ½ lime

pinch of salt

40g gluten-free plain white flour blend

1 lemon, cut into wedges, to serve

red onion marmalade (page 162), to serve

mango mayonnaise (page 159), to serve

seasonal salad leaves, to serve

FOR THE BATTER:

100g gluten-free plain white flour blend

80g gluten-free cornflour

pinch of bread soda

250ml sparkling water

½ tsp white wine vinegar

If entertaining guests, this recipe appeals to all.

Heat the oil in a deep-fat fryer until it reaches 190°C.

To make the batter, sieve the white flour blend, cornflour and a pinch of bread soda into a bowl and make a well in the centre. Pour in the sparkling water and vinegar and mix well with a whisk. Leave the batter to rest while you prepare the prawns.

Prepare the prawns by removing their head and shell from the tail (or ask your fishmonger to do this for you). Place in a large bowl with the coriander, lime zest and juice and a pinch of salt. Gently mix by hand until all the ingredients are incorporated.

Drain any excess liquid from the prawns, then sieve in the flour and mix gently, ensuring all the prawns are coated in the flour. Shake off any excess flour before adding the prawns to the batter.

Using a fork, carefully remove five prawns from the batter, shaking off the excess batter. Place the prawns in the deep-fat fryer and cook for 4 minutes, until golden brown. Set aside to drain on a plate lined with kitchen paper to absorb any excess grease. Repeat the process for all of the remaining prawns.

Serve immediately with lemon wedges, red onion marmalade, mango mayonnaise and seasonal salad leaves.

GET AHEAD

If you're entertaining and want to get a head start, the prawns can be prepared earlier in the morning with the coriander and lime etc. and left in the fridge. If you're serving it with the suggested accompaniments, these can be prepared well in advance too, which means you will only have to make the batter and cook the prawns when required.

bruschetta

SERVES 4

1 loaf of gluten-free bread or 2 gluten-free baps

1 garlic clove, cut in half

50ml good-quality extra virgin olive oil

salt and freshly ground black pepper

3 vine-ripened tomatoes

8 fresh basil leaves

20ml white wine vinegar

1 log of goats' cheese, cut into 1cm slices (optional)

green salad, to serve

Bruschetta toppings can be as humble or as luxurious as you like, from chopped fresh herbs or tomato with basil, to marinated vegetables or beautiful cheeses, to lovely flaked crabmeat. The only rule is that whatever goes on top of a bruschetta should be nice and fresh.

If you have a large loaf, cut it in half, then slice it crossways about 1cm thick. Chargrill the slices on a hot griddle pan until they are crisp on both sides, then lightly rub each piece a couple of times with the cut garlic clove. Drizzle with a little of the extra virgin olive oil and sprinkle with a tiny pinch of salt. You can eat the toasted bread just like this, but make sure the oil is of good quality, otherwise it will never taste nice.

Make sure your tomatoes are really ripe when making this topping. Give them a wash, then remove their cores by cutting them into quarters and removing the seeds. The tomatoes can either be left chunky or finely chopped.

Place the tomatoes in a bowl. Tear in the basil with your hands and season with salt and pepper, then toss with the remaining olive oil and the vinegar to balance the flavours to your taste.

You can spoon the tomato mixture onto the slices of bread and serve as is, or you can place the sliced goats' cheese on top of the tomato and bake the bruschetta in the oven or flash under the grill until the cheese has heated through and started to melt. Serve with a green salad.

crab cakes

MAKES 8 X 50G CRAB CAKES

300g crabmeat

100g cooked cold mashed potatoes

2 egg yolks

10g fresh coriander, chopped

10g fresh dill, chopped

¼ green chilli, deseeded and finely chopped

zest and juice of ½ lime

pinch of cayenne pepper

25ml olive oil

red onion marmalade (page 162), to serve

organic salad leaves, to serve

FOR THE COATING:

100g gluten-free plain white flour blend

salt and freshly ground black pepper

3 egg yolks

200ml milk

500g gluten-free breadcrumbs

There really is only one adaption made with this recipe, and that is the use of gluten-free flour and breadcrumbs. These crab cakes can also be pan-fried on their own without the crumb once the crab mix is good and dry. The secret of a good crab cake is that the crabmeat should be dry, with no excess liquid.

Preheat the oven to 180°C.

Put the crabmeat in a large bowl and carefully pick through it using your fingers, checking the meat for any shell or cartilage. Transfer the crabmeat from the bowl to a clean tea towel and squeeze any liquid from the meat.

Place the crabmeat back into a large bowl with the cold mashed potatoes, egg yolks, coriander, dill, chilli, lime zest and juice and a pinch of cayenne pepper and combine well. Roll the mixture into 8 x 50g balls between the palms of your hands.

To coat the crab cakes, first place the flour into a shallow rectangular dish and season with salt and pepper. Whisk the three egg yolks and milk together in a medium-sized bowl. Place the breadcrumbs in a shallow rectangular dish.

Put all eight crab cakes into the seasoned flour and evenly coat each one. Shake off any excess flour, then place them into the egg mixture and shake off any excess egg. Lastly, place the crab cakes into the breadcrumbs and evenly coat each one. Take the crab cakes out of the breadcrumbs one at a time and place on a clean work surface. Shape into cakes with two palette knives or by hand.

Put a heavy-based or non-stick frying pan over a medium to high heat, then drizzle in the olive oil. Add the crab cakes and cook for 3 minutes on each side, until light golden. Transfer the cakes to a baking sheet and bake in the oven for a further 5 minutes, until the crab cakes are heated all the way through. Serve two crab cakes per person with red onion marmalade and organic salad leaves.

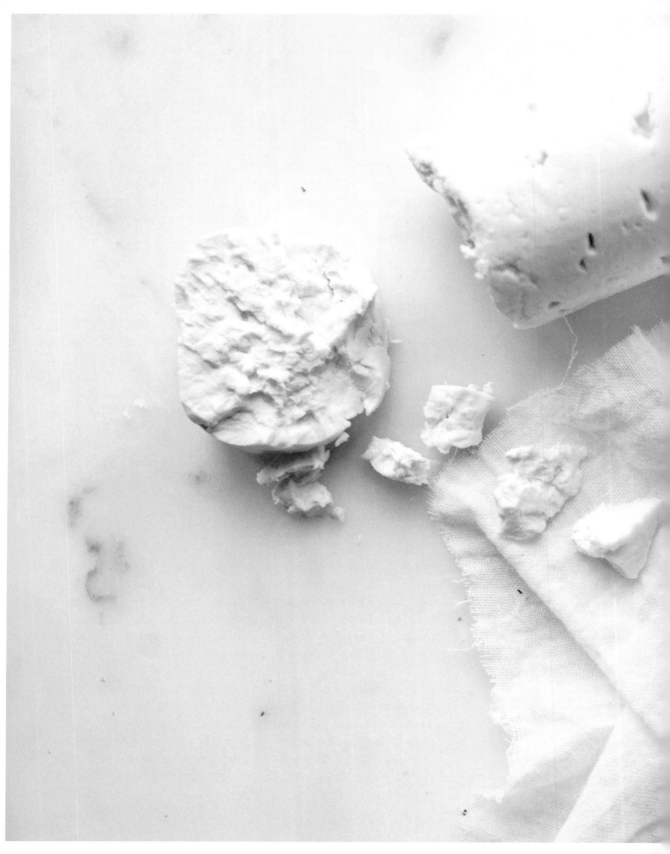

thai spiced fish cakes

MAKES 8 FISH CAKES

500g floury potatoes

1 litre fish stock (page 149)

200g salmon fillets, skinned and diced

200g cod fillets (or any white fish), skinned and diced

vegetable oil, for frying

4 spring onions, finely chopped

200ml coconut milk

2 tbsp Thai red curry paste

1 bunch of fresh coriander, finely chopped

zest and juice of 2 limes

salt and white pepper

200g gluten-free plain white flour blend

3 eggs, beaten

1 egg yolk, beaten

400g gluten-free breadcrumbs

lemon wedges, to serve

seasonal salad leaves, to serve

Fish cakes are a great way to use up leftovers and you can use whatever fish you like or is plentiful at the time. Adding a Thai dimension makes them a little more interesting.

Bring a large pan of salted water to the boil. Peel the potatoes and chop them into even-sized pieces. Add the potatoes to the water and bring it back to the boil. Cook for 10 minutes, until the potatoes are tender and cooked through. When the potatoes are done, drain them, mash and leave to cool.

In a separate pot, bring the fish stock to the boil and gently poach the diced pieces of salmon for 4–5 minutes. Remove the salmon and set aside, then add the diced pieces of cod to the stock for 3–4 minutes. Remove from the stock and leave to drain and cool.

Meanwhile, heat a little vegetable oil in a frying pan and cook the chopped spring onions for 2 minutes. Add the coconut milk and red curry paste and simmer for an additional 3 minutes.

When the mashed potatoes are cool, put them into a large bowl and flake the fish into it. Add the coconut milk mixture, the finely chopped coriander and the lime zest and juice and season with salt and white pepper. Mix together, but be careful not to overwork the mix.

Dust your work surface with a little flour. Divide the fish cake mixture into eight cakes about 1cm thick, dusting them with flour as you do. Place the beaten eggs and egg yolk in a shallow bowl. Place the breadcrumbs in a separate shallow dish.

Dip the fish cakes first into the beaten egg and then into the breadcrumbs to coat each of the fish cakes evenly. Place the coated fish cakes onto a tray, cover with cling film and rest for 30 minutes in the fridge.

Preheat the oven to 170°C.

To cook the fish cakes, heat a thin layer of vegetable oil in a frying pan over a medium heat. Add the fish cakes and fry for 3 minutes on each side, until golden brown. Transfer to a baking tray and bake in the oven for a further 5 minutes, until the fish cakes are heated all the way through. Place two fish cakes per person on a warmed plate and serve with a lemon wedge and seasonal salad leaves.

french onion soup

SERVES 4

40g butter

1 tsp olive oil

1kg onions, thinly sliced

50g dark brown sugar

4 garlic cloves, thinly sliced

2 sprigs of thyme, leaves picked

2 tbsp gluten-free plain white flour bend

250ml white wine

1.5 litres beef or chicken stock (page 148)

salt and freshly ground black pepper

4 slices of gluten-free bread

150g Gruyère or white Cheddar cheese, grated

There is no major adjustment required for French onion soup other than using gluten-free bread. It's a favourite of mine and is not complete without the croûte with melted cheese on top.

Melt the butter with the olive oil in a large heavy-based saucepan over a medium heat. Add the onions and sauté with the lid on for 8 minutes, then sprinkle in the brown sugar and cook, uncovered, for another 10 minutes. The onions should be golden brown and soft, but be careful not to burn them. Stir in the garlic, thyme and flour and cook for 2 minutes more.

Add the white wine and cook for a further 2 minutes, then add the stock and cover with a lid. Bring to the boil, then reduce the heat and simmer for 20 minutes. Taste the soup to correct the seasoning.

Grill the bread until toasted on each side. Ladle the soup into bowls and place a slice of the toasted bread on top. Sprinkle with lots of grated cheese and place under the grill for 2–4 minutes, until the cheese is melted and golden.

seafood chowder

SERVES 6

30g butter

1 tbsp olive oil

125g bacon, chopped

1 large onion, chopped

1 tbsp gluten-free plain white flour blend

300g potatoes, diced into 1cm pieces

800ml fish stock (page 149)

400g fish pieces (cod, salmon, smoked haddock, prawns and mussels)

25g fresh flat-leaf parsley, chopped

25g fresh dill, chopped

400ml milk

pinch of cayenne pepper

100ml cream

salt and freshly ground black pepper

chopped fresh chives, to garnish

crusty gluten-free bread, to serve

The secret to a good seafood chowder is not to overcook the fish or cook it at too high a temperature, and to use the freshest ingredients.

Heat the butter and oil in a large heavy-based saucepan over a medium heat. Add the chopped bacon and cook for 4 minutes, then add the chopped onion and cook for a further 4 minutes. At this stage the bacon should be cooked through and the onion should be soft.

Add the flour and stir constantly for 2 minutes to cook out the flour, ensuring there are no lumps, then add the potatoes and fish stock. Cover with a lid and bring to the boil, then reduce the heat and simmer for 15 minutes.

Add the fish, fresh herbs, milk and cayenne pepper and gently simmer for a further 4 minutes. Add the cream to the chowder and cook for a further 2 minutes. Taste to check the seasoning and adjust if required.

Ladle into warmed bowls and garnish with some chopped chives. Serve with crusty gluten-free bread.

chicken and celeriac soup

SERVES 4

2 boneless chicken thighs, skin on

10g butter

2 small potatoes, peeled and chopped

2 celery sticks, chopped

2 leeks, white part only, chopped

1 whole celeriac, peeled and chopped

25g fresh flat-leaf parsley, chopped

1 litre chicken stock (page 148)

salt and freshly ground black pepper

200ml cream

chopped fresh chives, to garnish

This flavoursome soup is perfect for small children, and a complete meal if you add potatoes or pasta and other root vegetables. The secret to this soup is to start with a good chicken stock, like the homemade one on page 148.

Preheat the oven to 180°C.

Place the chicken thighs on a baking tray and roast in the oven for about 25 minutes, until cooked through and tender.

Melt the butter in a large saucepan set over a medium heat, then sweat all the vegetables for 2–3 minutes, until soft and light golden in colour. Add the parsley, then pour in the stock. Bring to the boil, then cover the pan, reduce the heat and simmer for 30–35 minutes. Taste to check if seasoning is required and adjust accordingly. Blend the soup with a hand-held blender or liquidiser until it's completely smooth, with no lumps.

Remove the skin from the chicken thighs and chop the cooked chicken into small dice. Add it to the soup with the cream and serve in warmed bowls, garnished with chopped fresh chives.

courgette, potato, white irish cheddar and chive soup

SERVES 4–5

200g potatoes, peeled and cut into even pieces

1 litre vegetable or chicken stock (page 148)

500g courgettes, cut into even pieces

1 medium onion, cut into even pieces

1 celery stick, chopped

½ leek, white part only, cut into even pieces

1 bay leaf

100g white Irish Cheddar cheese, grated

salt and freshly ground black pepper

1 dessertspoon chopped fresh chives

Sometimes courgettes need other flavours to bring them along, as in this soup with the potato, Cheddar and chives. It is a complete soup that is filling, satisfying and very easy to make.

Place the potatoes and stock in a large heavy-based saucepan and bring to the boil. Reduce the heat, cover and simmer for 10 minutes. Add the courgettes, onion, celery, leek and bay leaf and cook for a further 8 minutes. Remove the saucepan from the heat, remove and discard the bay leaf and stir in 75g of the Cheddar cheese.

Using a hand-held blender, purée the soup for 2 minutes. Pass the soup through a fine-mesh sieve into a clean pot, return to the heat and taste to check the seasoning.

To serve, pour into warmed soup bowls and garnish with the remaining cheese and a sprinkle of chopped chives.

chicken caesar salad

SERVES 4

4 skinless, boneless chicken breasts

½ tsp rock salt

½ tsp cracked black pepper

1 tbsp olive oil

2 garlic cloves, left whole

2 sprigs of thyme

1 sprig of tarragon

4 heads of baby gem lettuce or cos leaves, washed, dried and separated

8 slices of pancetta, grilled until crisp

30g Parmesan shavings

FOR THE GLUTEN-FREE CROUTONS:

1 tbsp good-quality olive oil

1 garlic clove, left whole

1 sprig of thyme

10g butter

4 slices of gluten-free bread, diced

FOR THE DRESSING:

70g Parmesan cheese, grated

3 anchovies

2 garlic cloves, crushed

juice of 1 lemon

4 tbsp mayonnaise (page 159)

A chicken Caesar salad just isn't complete without croutons! They give the much-needed change in texture that's required in any salad.

Preheat the oven to 190°C.

Season the chicken breasts with the rock salt and pepper. Heat a large frying pan over a medium heat and drizzle the olive oil into the pan. Add the whole garlic cloves, thyme and tarragon and cook for 2 minutes. Remove the garlic and herbs from the pan, add the chicken breasts and cook for 2–3 minutes on each side, until golden brown. Transfer the chicken to a baking tray and cook in the oven for 35 minutes, until cooked through. Remove from the oven and allow to rest.

To prepare the croutons, you can use the same pan that the chicken was sealed in. Heat the pan over a medium heat again and drizzle with the tablespoon of olive oil. Add the whole garlic clove and thyme and cook for 2 minutes. Discard the garlic and herbs and add the butter. Once it has melted, add the diced bread and cook for 2–3 minutes, until all the butter has been absorbed. Place the croutons on a baking tray and bake in the oven for 5 minutes, until crisp and golden.

To make the dressing, place all the ingredients in a bowl. You can use a hand-held blender to mix everything together. Blend to either a rough or smooth consistency, whichever you prefer.

To serve, use a large bowl for mixing the leaves and dressing and divide between four serving bowls. Place slices of the cooked chicken and pancetta on top of the dressed leaves. Garnish with the croutons and Parmesan shavings and season to taste.

poached salmon and dill salad

SERVES 4

1 litre water

juice of ½ lemon

1 bay leaf

5 fennel seeds

pinch of rock salt

400g salmon fillet, skin and bones removed

25g fresh dill, chopped

1 tsp mayonnaise (page 159)

freshly ground black pepper

This is a handy sandwich filler or spooned onto a corn cake.

Put the water into a medium-sized saucepan. Add the lemon juice, bay leaf, fennel seeds and rock salt and bring to the boil. Add the salmon, then reduce the heat and simmer for 8 minutes, until the salmon is firm but with a little give. Remove the salmon from the water and set aside to cool.

Once it's cold, break up the salmon fillet into pieces and place in a bowl. Add the chopped dill, mayonnaise and seasoning and mix to combine, but do not overmix. Taste and correct the seasoning if necessary.

GET AHEAD

The poached salmon will keep for up to three days in a sealed container in the fridge.

the gf blt

SERVES 4

12 slices of streaky bacon

1 dessertspoon olive oil

8 slices of gluten-free soda bread (page 10), cut 1cm thick

50g butter, softened

2 tbsp mayonnaise (page 159)

200g seasonal leaves

4 ripe plum tomatoes, sliced

salt and freshly ground black pepper

At lunchtime, a BLT just cannot be beaten. Enjoy!

Grill the streaky bacon for 4 minutes on each side, until cooked through and a little crispy.

Heat a chargrill pan over a medium heat. Drizzle in half of the olive oil and add four slices of bread to the pan. Toast on each side for 2 minutes, until golden and crisp. Repeat with the remaining bread.

To assemble the BLT, butter each slice of bread, then spread each slice with mayonnaise.

Place the salad leaves on four slices of bread and top with sliced tomato. Put two slices of bacon on top of the tomato and lightly season with salt and pepper. Finish by placing the remaining slices of bread on top and cut diagonally. Press lightly and hold together with a cocktail stick.

chicken and chive salad

SERVES 4

2 boneless, skinless chicken breasts

salt and freshly ground black pepper

25g fresh chives, chopped

juice of ½ lemon

2 tbsp mayonnaise (page 159)

This salad can be made with leftover cooked chicken and is very tasty served on toasted gluten-free bread.

Preheat the oven to 190°C.

Place the chicken on a baking tray and season both sides of the breasts with salt and pepper. Roast the chicken in the oven for 35 minutes, until it's cooked all the way through, with no pink juices. Leave to cool.

Once cool, dice the chicken into small pieces. Put the chicken into a bowl with the chopped chives, lemon juice and mayonnaise and mix together. Taste and adjust the seasoning if necessary. It can be served as part of a salad or as a sandwich filler.

GET AHEAD

The salad will keep for up to three days in a sealed container in the fridge.

chargrilled chicken pasta salad

SERVES 4

4 skinless, boneless chicken breasts

salt and freshly ground black pepper

50ml olive oil

200g gluten-free pasta

2 medium onions, finely chopped

1 red pepper, finely chopped

2 garlic cloves, crushed

½ tsp cayenne pepper

1 courgette, cut into small dice

50g pine nuts

30g fresh basil leaves, torn

100g Parmesan cheese, grated

This is a simple yet tasty filler that's popular with everybody. You can tweak and change any of the ingredients, plus this is delicious served hot or cold.

Preheat the oven to 190°C.

Heat a griddle pan over a high heat. Season the chicken breasts with salt and pepper and lightly drizzle the pan with 1 teaspoon of the olive oil. Once the pan is hot, place the chicken breasts onto the pan and cook for 2 minutes on each side just to give it a charred appearance. Transfer to a baking tray and cook in the oven for a further 35 minutes, until cooked all the way through, with no pink flesh or juices. Once cooked, remove from the oven and allow it to rest while you prepare the rest of the salad.

Bring a large pot of salted water to the boil and cook the gluten-free pasta according to the packet instructions.

Heat the rest of the olive oil in a large, deep frying pan over a medium heat. Add the onions, red pepper, garlic and cayenne pepper and cook for 5 minutes. Add the courgette and cook for a further 2 minutes, then add the pine nuts and cook for 1 minute, being careful not to let them burn.

Add the cooked, drained pasta and fresh basil and cook for a further 3 minutes. Add the Parmesan, taste and correct the seasoning if required. Divide between four serving plates or bowls.

Carve each chicken breast into three, place on top of the pasta and serve.

GET AHEAD

The salad will keep for up to three days in a sealed container in the fridge.

mixed bean and sweet potato salad

SERVES 4–6

200g dried beans (any variety or a mix of white beans, black-eyed beans, butter beans or chickpeas), soaked separately overnight, or 1 x 400g tin of mixed beans, drained and rinsed

1 red pepper

2 sweet potatoes, peeled and sliced approx. 1cm thick

salt and freshly ground black pepper

40ml extra virgin olive oil

25g fresh basil leaves

¼ tsp chilli flakes

Like all the other salads in this chapter, this salad will keep in the fridge for up to three days in a sealed container and is handy to have ready if you have a busy schedule.

Preheat the oven to 240°C.

If using dried beans that have been soaked overnight, drain the water from the beans and cook over a medium heat until tender in a pot of seasoned water – this should take about 10–15 minutes. Once cooked, drain the water from the beans and leave to cool.

Meanwhile, place the whole red pepper on a small baking tray and roast in the oven for 30 minutes, until the pepper is tender and dark. Place in a bowl, cover tightly with cling film and set aside to cool for 20 minutes. This allows the skin to crease further and makes it easy to peel. Carefully remove the core of the pepper by the stalk, then begin to peel by hand, ensuring all the seeds are removed. Cut into even-sized pieces.

Reduce the oven temperature to 190°C. Place the sliced sweet potatoes on a baking tray, season with salt and pepper and drizzle with half of the olive oil. Bake in the oven for 15 minutes, until cooked through, then set aside to cool.

Once cool, put the sweet potatoes into a medium bowl with the cooked beans, chopped red pepper, basil leaves and chilli flakes. Mix together, drizzle with the remaining olive oil, taste and adjust the seasoning if required. Serve hot or cold on its own or with fish, chicken or turkey.

GET AHEAD

The salad will keep for up to three days in a sealed container in the fridge.

dinner

I WANTED TO make sure that I didn't miss out on old favourites such as chicken Kiev or bangers and mash, so I've reworked them as gluten-free versions. Cooking should be a pleasurable experience without being daunting, tedious or time consuming. From family meals to dinner parties, it's over the dinner table that people come together. These recipes will allow you to serve meals that everyone can enjoy.

chicken, pepper and tarragon casserole

SERVES 4

1 tbsp olive oil

8 chicken thighs, on the bone

2 medium onions, chopped

2 red peppers, diced

2 celery sticks, thinly sliced

1 carrot, chopped

2 garlic cloves, crushed

1 small slice of root ginger, peeled

600ml chicken stock (page 148)

2 small bunches of fresh tarragon, chopped

2 bay leaves

2 tbsp Dijon mustard

salt and freshly ground black pepper

rice or new potatoes, to serve

I use chicken thighs on the bone for a number of reasons: they are reasonably priced, have more flavour and are ultimately a better cut.

Preheat the oven to 180°C.

Heat the olive oil in a heavy-based casserole over a medium heat. Brown the chicken thighs until they are golden. This will seal in the juices, leaving the thighs full of flavour. Remove the browned chicken from the casserole and set aside.

Add the onions, peppers, celery and carrot to the casserole and cook for about 3 minutes, until soft, then add the garlic and ginger and cook for a further 2 minutes.

Add 100ml of stock to the vegetables and return the chicken to the casserole along with the tarragon, bay leaves and mustard. Add just enough of the remaining stock to the casserole to cover all the ingredients, then transfer to the oven and bake, uncovered, for 1 hour.

Take the casserole from the oven and place it on the hob. Remove the chicken again using a slotted spoon and set aside. At this point all of the ingredients will be cooked, but now you want to get a good sauce-like consistency with a nice sheen to the cooking liquor, so reduce the liquid on a high heat for 3 minutes, then taste and correct the seasoning. Return the chicken to the sauce, which should coat the chicken. Serve with rice or boiled new potatoes.

chicken curry

SERVES 4–6

4 chicken breasts or 10 chicken thighs, cut into bite-sized pieces

2 garlic cloves, crushed

½ fresh chilli, chopped, with seeds

10g fresh ginger, peeled and chopped

juice of 1 lime

1 tsp garam masala

salt and freshly ground black pepper

2 tbsp vegetable oil

2 large onions, finely chopped

100ml coconut milk

100ml chicken stock (page 148)

4 tsp gluten-free madras curry powder (medium hot)

1 tsp chopped fresh coriander

rice, to serve

Coeliacs can get caught out with a curry, as it often has thickening agents or other gluten products. This particular curry has a light consistency, as a curry should be, and is handy to have in your repertoire in terms of how quick and easy it is to make.

Place the chicken in a bowl with the crushed garlic, the chilli and its seeds, the ginger, lime juice and garam masala. Season with salt and mix well. Cover with cling film and place in the fridge for 1 hour to allow the flavours to infuse.

Heat the oil in a deep frying pan or saucepan over a medium heat. Add the onions and cook for 6–7 minutes, until soft and golden brown. Add the chicken and fry for 5 minutes, then add the coconut milk, stock and curry powder. Cover with a lid and leave to simmer gently for about 20 minutes.

Stir in the chopped coriander, taste to correct the seasoning and serve with rice.

chicken and mushroom casserole

SERVES 4

50g butter

200g streaky bacon, chopped

4 chicken breasts, cut into pieces

200g potatoes, peeled and cut into approx. 2cm cubes

150g onion, chopped

150g leek, white part only, chopped

2 celery sticks, chopped

1 bay leaf

300g button mushrooms, quartered

50g gluten-free plain white flour blend

1.25 litres hot chicken stock (page 148)

100ml cream

1 tbsp chopped fresh parsley

salt and freshly ground black pepper

rice or new potatoes, to serve

This chicken casserole is real comfort food, and one for all the family.

Melt the butter in a large pot over a medium heat, then add the bacon and cook for 2 minutes. Add the chicken and cook for a further 3–4 minutes without colouring it. Add the potatoes, onion, leek, celery and bay leaf. Continue to stir and cook for a further 4 minutes. Add the mushrooms and flour and mix well, then slowly add the hot chicken stock, stirring continuously. Bring to the boil, then reduce the heat to a simmer and cook for 20 minutes.

Add the cream and chopped parsley and cook for a further 2 minutes, then taste and season if required. Serve with rice or new potatoes.

GET AHEAD

This casserole can be made in advance and reheats well.

chicken cordon bleu

SERVES 4

4 chicken breasts

4 slices of cooked ham

4 slices of Emmental cheese

100g gluten-free plain white flour blend

½ tsp rock salt

¼ tsp ground white pepper

3 egg yolks

100ml milk

400g gluten-free herb breadcrumbs

sunflower oil, for frying

runner beans or new potatoes, to serve

There are no compromises in this classic chicken dish.

Preheat the oven to 170°C.

Fan out the centre of each chicken breast by cutting into the side. Put a slice of cooked ham and a slice of cheese into the pocket of the breast. Fold back the chicken breast to its original shape, completely encasing the ham and cheese. Refrigerate until required or use straight away.

Put the flour in a shallow dish and season it with the salt and white pepper. Whisk the egg yolks and milk together in a bowl. Place the breadcrumbs in a flat tray.

First place the stuffed chicken breasts into the flour, ensuring they are evenly coated, then shake off any excess flour. Next, dip the chicken into the egg mixture, coating the breasts well and again shaking off any excess liquid. Finally, place the chicken in the breadcrumbs, patting them in the crumbs to make sure they are evenly covered. Leave to rest for 10 minutes while you clean up.

Heat the oil in a large pan over a medium heat. Shallow-fry or pan-fry the chicken for 2–3 minutes, until golden, then place on a baking tray and cook in the oven for 40 minutes, until the chicken is an even golden brown colour, cooked all the way through with no pink in the centre, and the cheese has melted. Serve with runner beans or new potatoes.

GET AHEAD

If you want to be organised, the chicken can be prepared in advance, wrapped and even frozen until required. If freezing, remove it the night before you're going to cook it and defrost in the fridge.

chicken kiev

SERVES 4

4 chicken breasts

100g gluten-free plain white flour blend

½ tsp rock salt

¼ tsp ground white pepper

3 egg yolks

100ml milk

400g gluten-free herb breadcrumbs

sunflower oil, for frying

FOR THE GARLIC BUTTER:

80g butter, softened

25g fresh flat-leaf parsley

4 garlic cloves, peeled

½ tsp rock salt

¼ tsp ground white pepper

side salad or new potatoes, to serve

Preparation is key with this tasty chicken dish, but elements of it can be prepared days in advance. It's full of flavour, and if you love garlic, as I do, you have your fix.

Put the butter, parsley, garlic, rock salt and white pepper in a food processor and blend until smooth. Place a large sheet of cling film on the counter. Using a spatula, scrape the butter out of the food processor onto the sheet of cling film, then roll into a cylindrical sausage shape. Wrap tightly in the cling film and refrigerate until required.

Preheat the oven to 170°C. Fan out the centre of each chicken breast by cutting into the side. Put a 20g slice of the garlic butter into the pocket of each breast. Fold back the chicken breast to its original shape, completely encasing the butter. Refrigerate until required or use straight away.

Put the flour in a shallow dish and season it with the salt and white pepper. Whisk the egg yolks and milk together in a bowl. Place the breadcrumbs in a flat tray. First place the stuffed chicken breasts into the flour, ensuring they are evenly coated, then shake off any excess flour. Next, dip the chicken into the egg mixture, coating the breasts well and again shaking off any excess liquid. Finally, place the chicken in the breadcrumbs, patting them in the crumbs to make sure they are evenly covered. Leave to rest for 10 minutes while you clean up.

Heat the oil in a large pan over a medium heat. Shallow-fry or pan-fry the chicken for 2–3 minutes, until golden, then place on a baking tray and cook in the oven for 40 minutes, until the chicken is an even golden brown colour and is cooked all the way through with no pink in the centre. Serve with a side salad or new potatoes.

GET AHEAD

If you want to be organised, the chicken can be prepared in advance, wrapped and even frozen until required. If freezing, remove it the night before you're going to cook it and defrost in the fridge.

southern fried chicken

SERVES 6

12 chicken pieces, such as thighs, drumsticks, wings and breast, cut in half

600ml buttermilk

2 litres vegetable oil, for deep-frying

150g gluten-free plain white flour blend

80g cornflour

zest of 1 lemon

zest of 1 lime

2 tsp garlic powder

2 tsp chilli flakes

2 tsp black onion seeds

2 tsp dried sage

2 tsp dried oregano

2 tsp dried basil

2 tsp smoked paprika

2 tsp sweet paprika

2 tsp rock salt

2 tsp ground white pepper

corn on the cob, to serve

coleslaw, to serve

This is one of those dishes that anybody who is on a gluten-free diet truly misses, but it's actually quite simple to put together – it's just a matter of having the right ingredients at hand.

Place the chicken pieces in a large bowl with the buttermilk and mix by hand, ensuring the chicken is coated all over. Cover with cling film and refrigerate overnight.

Heat the oil in a deep-fat fryer to 180°C. Preheat the oven to 190°C.

Mix all the dry ingredients together in a large bowl. Remove the chicken pieces from the buttermilk, shaking off any excess, then toss the chicken in the dry ingredients, making sure all the chicken pieces are completely coated.

Working in batches, carefully place the chicken into the deep-fat fryer and cook for 5 minutes, until the coating is crisp. Transfer to kitchen paper to absorb any excess grease, then place on a baking tray and finish cooking the chicken in the oven for about 18 minutes, depending on the thickness of the chicken pieces.

Serve with corn on the cob and coleslaw.

traditional roast chicken and jus

SERVES 4–6

3 onions

2 carrots, chopped

½ leek, sliced

4 garlic cloves, peeled

1 bay leaf

sprig of thyme

1 x 1.5kg whole chicken

salt and freshly ground black pepper

FOR THE STUFFING:

100g butter

100g onion, chopped

50g celery, chopped

20g fresh sage, chopped

200g gluten-free breadcrumbs

20g fresh parsley, chopped

1 egg, beaten

FOR THE JUS:

100ml red wine

400ml chicken stock (page 148)

TO SERVE:

braised carrots with tarragon
(page 144)

red cabbage and apple (page 142)

gratin potato (page 147)

A whole roast chicken is a real family dinner with lots of memories attached. It requires a little effort and a bit of washing up afterwards, but it's well worth it.

Preheat the oven to 220°C.

Peel all three onions. Cut two of them into quarters and cut the last one in half. Place the quartered onions in a 30cm x 25cm roasting tin with the carrots, leek, garlic, bay leaf and thyme, then put the chicken on top of the vegetables. Season the chicken on the outside and season inside the cavity too, then place the remaining halved onion into the cavity. Roast the chicken in the oven for 15 minutes, then reduce the temperature to 180°C and cook for 1 hour more.

To make the stuffing, melt the butter in a large pot set over a medium heat. Add the onion, celery and sage and cook for 4 minutes, until the vegetables are soft. Add the breadcrumbs and parsley and stir for 2 minutes. Taste and adjust the seasoning and set aside.

Line a baking dish with a layer of tin foil followed by a layer of greaseproof paper spread out flat. Add the beaten egg to the stuffing and mix it through, then place the stuffing down the centre of the greaseproof paper. Fold or roll up the paper, making sure the stuffing is completely sealed within the paper. Seal the greaseproof paper with the tin foil that is wrapped around it. Put the stuffing into the oven for the final 20 minutes of the chicken roasting time.

To make sure the chicken is cooked, pierce a skewer into the thickest part of the thigh – the juices should be clear, with no trace of pink. If it is pink, return the chicken to the oven and cook a little longer. The cooked chicken should have crispy golden brown skin and the meat should be cooked all the way through.

To make the jus, remove the chicken from the roasting tin and place it on a large plate to rest, loosely covered with tin foil. Remove any excess fat from the roasting tin either by pouring it off (but without losing any of the juices in the tin) or simply remove by using a spoon.

Put the roasting tin onto the hob over a medium heat. Add the red wine and reduce by half, then add the chicken stock and reduce by half, stirring continuously. Pass the jus through a fine-mesh sieve into a small saucepan. Bring to the boil, taste and correct the seasoning.

Remove the tin foil from the chicken. Carve the chicken by removing the legs first, then separate the thigh from the leg. Carve the breast into slices. Serve the chicken with the stuffing and jus, along with braised carrots with tarragon, red cabbage and apple, and gratin potato.

roast chicken pieces, crushed potatoes and white wine cream

SERVES 4–6

10 medium potatoes, quartered or cut into large chunks

1 large chicken, jointed, or 8 chicken pieces on the bone

200g bacon, cut into lardons

2 onions, chopped

3 garlic cloves, chopped

2 sprigs of rosemary

2 sprigs of thyme

4 tbsp olive oil

salt and freshly ground black pepper

chopped fresh flat-leaf parsley

light summer salad, to serve

FOR THE WHITE WINE CREAM:

30g butter

3 shallots, finely diced

2 sprigs of thyme

150ml white wine

200ml cream

1 tbsp Dijon mustard

juice of ¼ lemon

This is a different take on a traditional roast that's quite handy and very tasty.

Preheat the oven to 200°C.

To parcook the potatoes, bring a medium-sized pot of lightly salted water to the boil, add the prepared potatoes, reduce the heat to medium and cook for approximately 5 minutes. Drain the potatoes, return them to the pan and press with the back of a spoon to crush them slightly.

Put the chicken pieces, bacon, onions, garlic and herbs in a roasting tin. Drizzle with olive oil and season with salt and pepper. Roast in the oven on a high heat for 20 minutes to crisp the chicken and bacon and give a good roasted flavour to the vegetables. After 20 minutes, reduce the oven temperature to 170°C. Add the par-cooked potatoes to the roasting tin and cook for 1 hour more. The chicken is cooked when the juices run clear when you pierce the thickest part of the thigh with a skewer. The skin should be crisp and the meat should be tender.

Meanwhile, to prepare the white wine cream, melt the butter in a medium-sized pot, then add the shallots and thyme and cook for 2 minutes, until the shallots are soft but not coloured. Add the white wine and bring to the boil, then reduce the liquid by half over a medium heat. Add the cream and mustard and simmer for 3 minutes, then finally add the lemon juice and a little salt and pepper to taste.

Pour the white wine cream over the chicken, bacon and vegetables, transfer to a serving dish and garnish with the chopped fresh parsley. Serve with a light summer salad.

pork shoulder with potato croquettes

SERVES 6–8

3 garlic cloves, crushed

½ red chilli, deseeded and chopped

zest and juice of 1 lemon

1 tbsp olive oil

1 tsp chopped fresh sage

1 tsp chopped fresh thyme

1 tsp black onion seeds

1 tsp paprika

1 tsp rock salt

3.5kg pork shoulder, boned and rolled (ask your butcher to do this for you)

30ml white wine vinegar

apple and Calvados sauce (page 155), to serve

FOR THE CROQUETTES:

20g butter

100g bacon rashers, cut into dice

6 scallions, finely chopped

1 apple, peeled, cored and finely diced

1 tsp chopped fresh sage

1 tsp chopped fresh thyme

700g cooked dry mashed potato

6 egg yolks

100g gluten-free plain white flour blend

200ml milk

500g gluten-free breadcrumbs

vegetable oil, for deep frying

Pork shoulder is an underutilised joint. When it's prepared correctly and cooked for the appropriate amount of time, it's meltingly tender and the crackling is amazing.

Preheat the oven to 220°C.

Mix the garlic, chilli, lemon zest and juice, olive oil, herbs, onion seeds, paprika and rock salt together in a bowl. Rub the mixture into the pork shoulder and massage for 5 minutes. Place the pork on a wire rack set in a roasting tray and roast in the oven for 40 minutes, then reduce the heat to 150°C and roast for 2½ hours more.

To achieve good crackling, turn the oven back up to 220°C. Remove the pork from the oven and brush the skin with the white wine vinegar. Return to the oven and roast for a further 30 minutes. The pork should be cooked all the way through and the skin will be crisp and golden brown. When the pork comes out of the oven, reduce the temperature again to 190°C.

Meanwhile, to make the croquettes, melt the butter in a large saucepan over a medium heat, then add the bacon and cook for 5 minutes without colouring it. Add the scallions, apple, sage and thyme and cook for a further 2 minutes, then remove from the heat and allow to cool. Once cooled, add the cooked dry mashed potatoes and three egg yolks and mix until combined. Divide the mixture into 8 x 100g cylinders.

Place the flour in a shallow dish. Mix the remaining three egg yolks and the milk together in a bowl. Place the breadcrumbs in a separate shallow dish.

First place the croquettes in the flour, tossing to coat them well and shaking off any excess. Next, dip the croquettes into the egg mixture, again shaking off any excess, then finally place in the breadcrumbs, making sure they are evenly coated and again tapping off any excess crumbs.

Heat the vegetable oil in a deep-fat fryer or a large frying pan until it reaches 180°C. Fry the croquettes until they are golden brown, then set on a plate lined with kitchen paper to absorb any excess grease. Transfer to a baking tray and finish cooking in the oven for 5 minutes at 190°C.

To serve, remove the crackling simply by pulling it away from the meat and breaking the crackling into pieces. Use a carving knife to cut the pork into 1cm-thick slices. Serve with the apple and Calvados sauce and the potato croquettes.

GET AHEAD

You can rub the spice mixture into the pork shoulder the night before you want to cook it.

roast duck with cranberry and sage stuffing

SERVES 4

1 x 2kg whole duck

1 orange, cut in half

1 lemon, cut in half

2 sprigs of thyme

FOR THE STUFFING:

100g butter

80g onion, chopped

40g fresh cranberries

1 tsp chopped fresh sage

100g gluten-free breadcrumbs

salt and freshly ground black pepper

Roast duck is a very rich meat that can be a little messy in the oven – as it has a high fat content, it tends to spit, leaving you with a little extra clean-up. But if you're entertaining, your guests will really appreciate the effort. Roast duck is wonderful served with the red cabbage and apple on page 142, the gratin potatoes on page 147 and the bread sauce on page 155. And don't discard the fat from the roasting tray! It's fantastic for roasting potatoes and root vegetables.

Preheat the oven to 220°C.

Melt the butter in a medium-sized pot over a low heat. Add the chopped onion and cook slowly for 5 minutes. Add the cranberries and sage and cook for a further 3 minutes, then add the breadcrumbs and mix well. Taste and season accordingly.

Place the duck on a wire rack set on a baking tray. Fill the neck of the duck with the stuffing, then place the orange, lemon and sprigs of thyme into the cavity of the duck. Using butcher string, tie the legs together and around the parson's nose. This helps the duck to roast more evenly, as the legs won't cook as quickly this way.

Roast for 40 minutes, then reduce the heat to 190°C for a further 1 hour 20 minutes, basting occasionally with the fat in the tray. When cooked, the skin should be quite crisp from the basting and the meat should be cooked all the way through. You can check this by piercing the thickest part of the thigh with a knife or skewer – the juices should run clear.

To serve, it can be carved just like a roast chicken with the cranberry stuffing alongside.

white bean and sausage casserole

SERVES 4

1 tbsp olive oil

1 medium onion, chopped

8 good gluten-free butcher sausages (approx. 600g)

3 mixed peppers, roughly chopped

1 celery stick, chopped

4 garlic cloves, crushed

1 tsp chopped fresh thyme

1 tsp paprika

1 tsp cayenne pepper

150ml white wine

2 x 400g tins of chopped tomatoes

100ml chicken stock (page 148)

1 x 400g tin of white beans, drained and rinsed

salt and freshly ground black pepper

fresh rosemary, to garnish

gluten-free soda bread (page 10), to serve

This is a wholesome, tasty, filling meal that can be prepared in advance, which is especially handy if you're pressed for time. It's also great served with the toasted soda bread on page 10.

Heat the olive oil in a large heavy-based pot over a medium heat. Add the onion and cook for about 4 minutes, until soft. Add the sausages and cook for a further 5 minutes, then add the peppers, celery, garlic, thyme, paprika and cayenne pepper and cook for 5 minutes more.

Pour in the white wine and reduce by half. Add the chopped tomatoes and stock and almost bring to the boil, then reduce the heat and simmer for 30 minutes. Add the beans and cook for a further 8 minutes. Taste to check the seasoning and adjust if required. Garnish with fresh rosemary and serve with gluten-free soda bread.

GET AHEAD

This cassoulet can be prepared in advance and reheated when needed. Or you can prepare the vegetables the evening before, cover them well and store them in the fridge, and then it's just a case of cooking everything the next day.

bacon and cabbage terrine with leek cream

This is one of my favourite starters that we serve at The Olde Post Inn and is one of those dishes that I can't take off the menu. It can be a little tricky to prepare, but as long as it's pressed correctly, it works.

MAKES 10 PORTIONS

2 ham hocks

1 bay leaf

1 star anise

1 head of Savoy cabbage, cored and thinly sliced

FOR THE LEEK CREAM:

50g butter

1 small onion, chopped

1 celery stick, chopped

½ leek, white part only, chopped

800ml cream

2 star anise

2 cardamom seeds

2 white peppercorns

1 bay leaf

salt and ground white pepper

1 tbsp chopped fresh chives

Place the ham hocks in a large pot with the bay leaf and star anise. Cover with water and bring to the boil, then reduce the heat and simmer for 3 hours, until the meat is falling off the bone. Remove the hocks from the cooking liquor using a slotted spoon and let them cool slightly, retaining the cooking liquor but discarding the bay leaf and star anise. Pick the meat off the bones and remove any gristle or fat.

Prepare two terrine tins or two 2lb loaf tins by lining them with several layers of cling film, letting the excess hang over the sides of the tin in order to wrap up the contents later on.

Blanch the prepared cabbage by boiling it in the cooking liquor from the ham hocks for 3–5 minutes. Once cooked, strain the cabbage but still keep the cooking liquor for setting the terrine.

Fill the tin with alternating layers of ham and cabbage until the contents sit over the top of the tin by 2.5cm. Pour the cooking liquor over the terrine, ensuring the last layer is covered. Wrap the terrine with the overhanging cling film, keeping it tight.

Place the tins on a baking tray and refrigerate overnight with a heavy weight placed on top of each tin to press the terrine, making sure the tins are level. It is very important that the terrine is firm and set before removing it from the tin – it can take up to 24 hours to set properly.

To prepare the leek cream sauce, melt the butter in a medium-sized saucepan over a medium heat. Sweat the onion, celery and leek for about 5 minutes, then add the cream, star anise, cardamom, white peppercorns and bay leaf. Bring to the boil, then reduce the heat to low and simmer for 5 minutes.

Remove from the heat and allow to stand for 15 minutes, then pass through a fine-mesh sieve and discard the solids. Taste to correct the seasoning with salt and ground white pepper, then stir in the chopped chives and keep warm.

To serve, preheat the oven to 175°C. Cut the terrine with a sharp knife into slices 2cm thick and place on a baking tray. Cook in the oven for 3–4 minutes, until it is only just warm, not overheated, or it will fall apart. Place a slice of the terrine on a warmed plate and spoon over some of the leek cream.

GET AHEAD

This terrine is suitable for freezing after cutting into slices and wrapping individually in cling film.

roast leg of lamb with lamb jus

SERVES 6–8

1 x 2.5kg leg of lamb, on the bone

5 garlic cloves, crushed

30g fresh rosemary, chopped

20g fresh mint, chopped

50ml olive oil, plus extra for frying

1 tsp rock salt

3 carrots, peeled and cut down the centre

2 medium onions, peeled and cut in half

1 leek, white part only, roughly chopped

150ml red wine

1 litre lamb or chicken stock (page 148)

By cooking the lamb on the bone, you're getting all the juices needed to make a good jus. It's just a matter of following the steps and the results are delicious.

Make criss-cross cuts on the leg of lamb with a sharp knife. Mix the crushed garlic, rosemary, mint, olive oil and rock salt in a bowl, then rub this mix into the lamb. For the best result, wrap the lamb in cling film and refrigerate it overnight.

One hour before you intend to cook the lamb, remove it from the fridge to bring it to room temperature. Preheat the oven to 190°C.

Heat some olive oil in a large frying pan over a high heat and brown the leg of lamb all over. Place the carrots, onions and leek into the roasting tin and put the sealed leg of lamb on top. Roast in the oven for 1 hour 45 minutes, until the skin is crisp and puffed and the meat is pink. Loosely cover the lamb with tin foil and allow to rest for 30 minutes.

To make the jus, place the roasting tray on the hob over a medium heat. Add the red wine and reduce by half, then add the stock. Bring to the boil, then reduce the heat to a simmer for 5 minutes. Skim the top of the sauce to remove any impurities. At this stage, carefully pass the jus into a medium-sized pot through a fine-mesh sieve and reduce by half. The jus should be rich and slightly thick with a lovely lamb flavour.

To serve, carve the lamb into slices and spoon over the warm jus.

roast shoulder of lamb with summer vegetables and quinoa

SERVES 6

2 garlic cloves, finely chopped

1 tbsp olive oil

2 tsp cumin seeds

salt and freshly ground black pepper

1 x 1.4kg shoulder of lamb, boned and tied (ask your butcher to do this for you)

400g pearl onions or shallots, peeled and left whole

2 celery sticks, chopped

½ leek, white part only, chopped

500ml lamb stock

1 dessertspoon honey

SUMMER VEGETABLES AND QUINOA:

100g quinoa

700ml water

100g carrots, thinly sliced

100g fresh broad beans, podded and individually peeled

8 asparagus spears, ends snapped off

½ courgette, thinly sliced

1 tbsp roughly chopped fresh mint

This is a perfect Sunday lunch and will be a favourite with all the family. Shoulder of lamb is an economical cut of meat and it's incredibly tasty. Quinoa is a grain grown for its seeds and is a versatile and nutritious alternative to barley.

Preheat the oven to 140°C. Mix the garlic, olive oil and cumin seeds with some salt and pepper in a small bowl. Pour this over the lamb and rub it into the meat.

Place the lamb in a deep casserole with the onions, celery and leek and pour over the stock. Cover with a tight-fitting lid and cook in the oven for 3 hours, until the lamb is cooked through and soft to touch. Remove the casserole from the oven. Take the lamb out of the dish, place it in a roasting tin and glaze with the honey. Reserve the cooking liquor in the casserole dish.

Increase the oven temperature to 180°C. Return the lamb to the oven for 15–20 minutes to crisp it up. Remove the lamb from the oven, loosely cover with tin foil and leave to rest.

Meanwhile, rinse the quinoa well and place it in a saucepan with the water and a pinch of salt. Bring to the boil and cover with a lid, then reduce the heat and gently simmer for 10 minutes, until the grain unwinds. Turn off the heat and leave to cool slightly, then drain off any remaining water and fluff up the quinoa with a fork. Season with salt and pepper and set aside.

Using a large spoon, remove any surface fat from the top of the cooking liquor in the casserole. Add the carrots, broad beans, asparagus and courgette slices and return to the hob to heat for 3 minutes. Add the quinoa and chopped mint and stir to combine.

Transfer the quinoa and vegetables to a large warmed serving dish. Remove the string from the lamb and carve into thick slices. Sit the lamb on top of the bed of vegetables and quinoa and serve.

lamb's liver with red wine vinegar and sticky onions

SERVES 4

3 tbsp olive oil

100g butter

6 medium onions, sliced

700g lamb's liver, thinly sliced

6 tbsp red wine vinegar

100ml red wine

salt and freshly ground black pepper

mashed potatoes, to serve

Spring is the best time for buying and cooking lamb's liver, which is nicely contrasted here by the sweet onion and the sharp vinegar.

Heat the olive oil and half of the butter in a heavy-based saucepan over a low heat. Add the sliced onions and cook them slowly for at least 30 minutes, allowing them to soften and colour. The longer the onions cook without burning, the better – this results in a better caramelisation. Remove the onions from the pan and keep them warm by placing them on a plate and covering it with tin foil.

With the pan still on the hob over a low heat, add the remaining butter. When the butter is hot, add the lamb's liver and cook over a high heat. Do not move the liver until it's golden brown. This allows the liver to seal and should only take a minute. Turn the liver over and cook for a further minute. Remove the liver from the pan and keep warm.

With the pan still on a high heat on the hob, pour in the red wine vinegar, letting it sizzle. Scrape up any browned bits from the bottom of the pan, then add the red wine along with some salt and pepper.

Return the onions to the frying pan and stir. Place the liver on top and cook at a high heat for 1 minute. When everything is warmed through, remove the liver from the pan, pour the contents of the pan over the liver and serve immediately with mashed potatoes and the sticky onions.

risotto

SERVES 4

1.5 litres chicken stock (page 148)

110ml olive oil

3 shallots, finely diced

2 garlic cloves, chopped

300g Arborio rice

100ml white wine

150g Parmesan cheese, grated

40g salted butter, cut into cubes

1 bunch of chives, finely chopped

salt and ground white pepper

This basic risotto can be adapted by adding different flavours, meats or fish. Risotto is particularly good served as an accompanying dish with fish or chicken. A good stock in any risotto adds a rich flavour.

Bring the stock to the boil and set aside, keeping it warm.

Heat the oil in a heavy-bottomed pan over a low heat. Add the shallots and cook for 1 minute, until soft. Add the garlic and cook for another 2 minutes, then add the rice and cook for 2 minutes more. This helps to add flavour to the rice. Pour in the white wine and briefly increase the heat to burn off the alcohol.

Add a ladleful of the warm stock and cook over a medium heat, stirring frequently and topping up with sufficient warm stock as it is absorbed to ensure the rice is always just covered. This should take 20–25 minutes.

Add half of the Parmesan, the cubed butter and the chopped chives. Stir and season to taste.

Divide between four warmed plates, sprinkle with the remaining Parmesan and serve straight away.

smoked haddock risotto with parmesan

SERVES 4–6

1.5 litres fish stock (page 149)

110ml olive oil

3 shallots, finely diced

2 garlic cloves, chopped

300g Arborio rice

100ml white wine

200g cooked smoked haddock

150g Parmesan cheese, grated

40g salted butter, cut in cubes

1 bunch of chives, finely chopped

salt and ground white pepper

This dish is ideal for a light lunch or supper and the fish stock adds a rich flavour. To make this a heartier meal, add a poached egg on top to finish.

Bring the stock to the boil and set aside, keeping it warm.

Heat the oil in a heavy-bottomed pan over a low heat. Add the shallots and cook for 1 minute, until soft. Add the garlic and cook for another 2 minutes, then add the rice and cook for 2 minutes more. This helps to add flavour to the rice. Pour in the white wine and briefly increase the heat to burn off the alcohol.

Add a ladleful of the warm stock and cook over a medium heat, stirring frequently and topping up with sufficient warm stock as it is absorbed to ensure the rice is always just covered. This should take 20–25 minutes.

Flake the smoked haddock into pieces and add to the risotto along with half of the Parmesan, the cubed butter and the chopped chives. Stir and season to taste.

Divide between four warmed plates, sprinkle with the remaining Parmesan and serve straight away.

mussels with white wine, cream, garlic and parsley

SERVES 4

15g butter

300g baby leeks, chopped

2 onions, finely chopped

2 garlic cloves, finely chopped

2.5kg mussels, beards removed and scraped clean

450ml white wine

650ml cream

salt and freshly ground black pepper

1 bunch of fresh flat-leaf parsley, chopped

gluten-free soda bread (page 10), to serve

Mussels can be served at any time of the day or evening, and sometimes there is nothing like eating with your hands. What a flavoursome and simple dish.

Melt the butter in a large saucepan set over a low heat. Sweat the leeks, onions and garlic for 4 minutes, then add the mussels and white wine and cover the pan with a lid. Cook on a high heat for 8–10 minutes, until all the mussels have opened. Stir them once or twice as they cook to rotate the mussels and to ensure they are all evenly cooked. Remove the mussels from the saucepan, discarding any unopened ones, and set aside.

Strain the cooking liquid into a clean saucepan through a fine-mesh sieve and add the cream. Bring to the boil, then reduce the heat and simmer for 5–6 minutes. Return the mussels to the pan and season if necessary.

Add the chopped fresh parsley and serve the mussels and cooking liquor in a warmed shallow bowl with toasted gluten-free soda bread.

chicken, chorizo and prawn paella

SERVES 6

5 tbsp olive oil

3 medium onions, finely chopped

3 garlic cloves, crushed

900g boneless, skinless chicken breasts or thighs, cut into bite-sized pieces

150g gluten-free chorizo sausage, skin removed and cut into 1cm-thick slices

125g tinned butter beans, drained and rinsed

1 tbsp paprika

1 tsp saffron

salt and freshly ground black pepper

800g long-grain rice

2 litres warm chicken stock (page 148)

4 ripe tomatoes

12 fresh or frozen king prawns, tails only and shells removed

100g peas

15g fresh flat-leaf parsley (about 2 handfuls), roughly chopped

This one-pot wonder is a real crowd pleaser and very convenient if you're entertaining, as you can just pop it on the table for everyone to help themselves. The basic paella ingredients are rice, saffron and olive oil, but you can vary the other ingredients any way you wish.

Heat the olive oil in a large heavy-based pan over a medium heat. Add the onions and garlic and cook for 1 minute, then add the prepared chicken and chorizo and cook just until sealed. Add the butter beans, paprika and saffron and lightly season with salt and pepper.

Add the rice and stir well, then add the warm chicken stock and cook on a low heat for 20 minutes, until all the stock has been absorbed and the flavour has infused the rice. Stir the rice regularly to make sure it isn't sticking to the bottom of the pan.

While the rice is cooking, prepare the tomatoes. Remove the green core with a pointed sharp knife and make a cross on the opposite side, just cutting through the skin. Bring a medium-sized saucepan half-filled with water to the boil. Add the tomatoes to the boiling water and leave on a high heat for 10 seconds (although this depends on how ripe the tomatoes are). Remove the tomatoes from the boiling water with a slotted spoon and plunge into a bowl of ice-cold water to refresh the tomato. Once cold, the tomatoes should peel easily. Cut into quarters and remove the seeds. The flesh of the tomato should still hold its structure. Cut into even-sized dice.

When the rice is done, add the prawns, tomatoes and peas to the paella, remove the pan from the heat, cover it with a lid and leave to sit for 5 minutes – the residual heat will be enough to cook the prawns. Sprinkle the parsley all over the rice and serve.

fish pie

SERVES 4

300ml white wine

250ml water

150ml white wine vinegar

150g salmon, cubed

150g haddock or cod, cubed

150g fresh or frozen prawns

250ml milk

150g smoked haddock or cod, cubed

1 litre fish stock (page 149)

400ml cream

salt and ground white pepper

1 bunch of chives, chopped

400g mashed potatoes

fresh garden peas, to serve

braised carrots with tarragon (page 144), to serve

There are two components to this dish: cooking the unsmoked fish and shellfish in white wine and cooking the smoked fish in the milk, then combining the two in a creamy fish sauce. Any fish or shellfish can be used in this pie.

Preheat the oven to 200°C.

Bring the white wine, water and vinegar to the boil in a medium-sized saucepan, then reduce the heat to medium and add the unsmoked fish and prawns. Poach for 6 minutes, until the fish is just cooked. Remove from the liquid and allow to cool. Discard the cooking liquid.

Heat the milk in a separate saucepan until it's just about to boil and poach the smoked fish for 6 minutes, until cooked, then remove from the heat and allow to cool. Take the smoked fish out of the milk, combine with the other poached fish and divide between four individual ovenproof dishes. Discard the milk.

Meanwhile, make the sauce by reducing the fish stock in a small saucepan by half, then adding the cream, reducing the heat and simmering for 10 minutes, until it's smooth and coats the back of the spoon. Season to taste and allow to cool slightly.

Pour the sauce over the fish in the ovenproof dishes and sprinkle with chopped chives. If you have a piping bag, pipe the mashed potato on top of the fish. Alternatively, spoon the mashed potato on top, spread it out evenly with the back of the spoon and run the tines of a fork through the potatoes so that they crisp up in the oven.

Cook for 25–30 minutes, until the pie is heated through and the potatoes are golden and crisp on top. Serve with fresh garden peas and braised carrots with tarragon.

traditional fish and chips

SERVES 4

vegetable oil, for frying

150g gluten-free plain white flour blend

zest of 1 lemon

2 sprigs of fresh dill, chopped

salt and freshly ground black pepper

4 x 180g pieces of whatever white fish is in season, boned (ask your fishmonger to do this for you)

tartare sauce (page 167), to serve

lemon wedges, to serve

FOR THE BATTER:

80g gluten-free plain white flour blend

80g cornflour

¼ tsp gluten-free baking powder

160ml gluten-free lager

¼ tsp white wine vinegar

FOR THE HOME-CUT CHIPS:

8 large Maris Piper potatoes

There is something special about a good fish and chips. The key is a crisp batter, fresh fish and a floury potato. I think you'll find that this recipe is even better than its usual alternative.

Place the flour blend, cornflour and baking powder in a large bowl and mix together, then make a well in the centre. Add the beer and vinegar, season with a little salt and pepper and whisk to combine into a batter. Leave to rest for 1 hour in the fridge or you could even make the batter the day before you need it.

While the batter is resting, peel the potatoes and cut them into even rectangular chips. Steam the chips for 8 minutes in a steamer or in a colander set over a pot of boiling water. Once the chips are slightly tender, remove them from the heat and leave to cool.

Heat the oil in a deep-fat fryer until it reaches 180°C. Preheat the oven to 130°C.

To prepare the fish, place the flour in a large, shallow dish with the lemon zest, dill and seasoning. Coat the fish in the flour and shake off any excess. Next, coat the fish in the batter and gently lower it into the fryer, placing the fish away from you.

Cook for 6–8 minutes, depending on how thick the fish is. The cooked fish must be moist and slightly undercooked and the batter should be quite crisp. Transfer to a baking tray and keep the fish warm in the oven while you cook the chips.

To finish cooking the chips, bring the fryer back up to 180°C, add the chips and cook for 5 minutes, until they are crisp and golden with a fluffy texture in the centre. Drain on kitchen paper and season.

Serve the fish and chips with tartare sauce and a lemon wedge.

GET AHEAD

You could make the batter one day in advance.

herb-crusted hake with lemon cream

SERVES 4

4 x 180g hake fillets, skin on and deboned

salt and freshly ground black pepper

100g gluten-free breadcrumbs

zest of ½ lemon

zest of ½ lime

1 tsp chopped fresh dill

1 tsp chopped fresh chives

1 tsp chopped fresh parsley

1 tsp thyme leaves

1 egg yolk

FOR THE LEMON CREAM:

200ml fish stock (page 149)

juice of 2 lemons

80ml cream

50g butter, cubed

This is a very light, fresh-tasting, simple and versatile way of serving most white fish. You can use cod, haddock, brill or turbot as an alternative to the hake and the sauce is wonderful with any fish too.

Preheat the oven to 190°C. Lightly oil a baking tray.

Place the hake fillets on the oiled baking tray, skin side down, and season lightly with salt and pepper.

Mix together the breadcrumbs, lemon and lime zest and all the fresh herbs in a bowl.

Place the egg yolk in a cup and beat with a fork. Dip a pastry brush into the beaten egg and brush it over the hake fillets. Sprinkle the crumb mixture over each of the fillets, then put the tray into the oven and bake for 8 minutes to crisp the crust. Reduce the heat to 160°C and cook for a further 5 minutes, until the hake is golden brown and slightly firm to the touch.

To make the lemon cream, place the fish stock and lemon juice in a medium-sized saucepan set over a high heat. Reduce the liquid by half, then add the cream and bring the sauce almost to the boil. Reduce the heat and slowly add the butter little by little. When all the butter has been fully incorporated, cook for a further 2 minutes and taste to correct the seasoning if required.

Serve the hake fillets on warmed plates with a little lemon cream spooned over.

cod with a bacon and cabbage cream

This cod dish is relatively straightforward to cook and prepare and there is very little washing up afterwards. The one thing to bear in mind when it comes to cod is the size of the fillets – they can be either quite thick or very thin, so the cooking times will vary.

Season the cod fillets on both sides with salt and pepper. Place a large frying pan over a high heat. Once it's hot, add a small knob of the butter and the olive oil. Add the cod to the pan, skin side down, then reduce the heat slightly. Cook for 4 minutes, then carefully turn the cod over and cook for a further 4 minutes. Remove the cod from the pan and leave to one side.

Raise the heat again, add the rest of the butter and cook the bacon pieces for 3 minutes. Add the lemon juice and fish stock and reduce the liquid by half. Add the cabbage and cream and bring to a simmer. Return the cod to the pan and cook for a further 3 minutes. Taste to check for seasoning and serve immediately, garnished with the chopped fresh dill. Serve with new potatoes.

SERVES 4

4 x 180g cod fillets, skin on and deboned

salt and freshly ground black pepper

50g butter

20ml olive oil

120g streaky bacon, chopped

juice of 1 lemon

200ml fish stock (page 149)

50g Savoy cabbage, white parts only, finely shredded

100ml cream

1 tsp chopped fresh dill

new potatoes, to serve

cod with chickpeas and chorizo

SERVES 4

4 x 180g cod fillets, skin on and deboned

salt and freshly ground black pepper

50g butter

20ml olive oil

100g gluten-free chorizo, cut into 1cm cubes

2 shallots, sliced

50ml white wine

juice of 1 lemon

200ml fish stock (page 149)

1 x 400g tin of chickpeas, drained and rinsed

100ml cream

1 tsp chopped fresh chives

new potatoes, to serve

seasonal greens, to serve

This is a variation on the cod with a bacon and cabbage cream on page 104. Cod or white fish in general is so versatile that it works with many different ingredients, herbs and spices, like the chickpeas and chorizo in this dish.

Season the cod fillets on both sides with salt and pepper. Place a large frying pan over a high heat. Once it's hot, add a small knob of the butter and the olive oil. Add the cod to the pan, skin side down, then reduce the heat slightly. Cook for 4 minutes, then carefully turn the cod over and cook for a further 4 minutes. Remove the cod from the pan and leave to one side.

Add the rest of the butter and the chorizo to the pan and cook for 3 minutes, then add the shallots and cook for a further 2 minutes. Add the white wine and lemon juice and cook for 1 minute more.

Add the fish stock and reduce by half, then add the chickpeas and cream and bring almost to the boil. Return the cod to the pan and cook for a further 3 minutes. Stir in the chives and taste to check for seasoning. Serve with new potatoes and seasonal greens.

fillet of cod with asparagus and sauce vierge

SERVES 4

12 asparagus spears

20ml olive oil

4 x 200g cod fillets, skin on and deboned

salt and ground white pepper

30g butter

25ml lemon juice

FOR THE SAUCE VIERGE:

100ml good-quality olive oil

3 shallots, finely chopped

25ml lemon juice

10 fresh basil leaves, cut into strips

1 tsp coriander seeds, crushed

3 tomatoes

This dish is a real favourite of mine in the summertime when all the ingredients are at their freshest. The sauce vierge is a wonderful fresh sauce to serve with most white or oily fish.

To make the sauce vierge, gently heat the oil in a medium-sized saucepan. Cook the shallots and lemon juice until the shallots are tender, then remove from the heat. Add the basil and coriander seeds and leave to infuse the warm oil for a few minutes.

Meanwhile, to prepare the tomatoes, remove the green core with a pointed sharp knife and make a cross on the opposite side, just cutting through the skin. Bring a medium-sized saucepan half-filled with water to the boil. Add the tomatoes to the boiling water and leave on a high heat for 10 seconds (although this depends on how ripe the tomatoes are). Remove the tomatoes from the boiling water with a slotted spoon and plunge into a bowl of ice-cold water to refresh the tomato. Once cold, the tomatoes should peel easily. Cut into quarters and remove the seeds. The flesh of the tomato should still hold its structure. Cut into even-sized dice. Add the diced tomatoes to the warm oil and set aside until required.

To prepare the asparagus, snap the tough ends off the spears (approx. 4–5cm off the ends), then carefully peel the ends of the stalk without removing too much actual asparagus.

Heat the olive oil in a frying pan until it's hot. Season the cod fillets on both sides with salt and pepper and place in the pan, skin side down. Reduce the heat to low and cook the fish for 3 minutes. Add the butter to the pan, turn the fish over and cook for another 3 minutes, spooning the butter over the fish occasionally. Finally, add the lemon juice.

Meanwhile, cook the asparagus in a large saucepan of boiling salted water for approximately 2 minutes. There should still be a bit of bite in the asparagus (al dente).

To serve, divide the asparagus between four warmed plates (three spears on each plate). Place the cod on top, skin side up, spoon the warm sauce vierge around the fillets and serve immediately.

curry seasoned monkfish

SERVES 4

4 x 180g monkfish fillets, bones and skin removed

50g gluten-free curry powder

50g butter

2 tomatoes

200ml fish stock (page 149)

juice of 1 lemon

8 cardamom seeds, crushed

100ml cream

2 tsp chopped chives

This is quite a special dish that would be suitable for entertaining. The secret is to make sure that you use very fresh fish that is well trimmed – your fishmonger can do this for you. And as with any fish, it's also important not to overcook it.

Preheat the oven to 180°C.

Place the monkfish fillets in a bowl and sprinkle with the curry powder. Heat a large frying pan over a high heat, then add the monkfish and a knob of the butter to the pan. Cook until golden brown all over, which should take 3–4 minutes. Remove from the pan, transfer to a baking tray and place in the oven for 8 minutes.

Meanwhile, to prepare the tomatoes, remove the green core with a pointed sharp knife and make a cross on the opposite side, just cutting through the skin. Bring a medium-sized saucepan half-filled with water to the boil. Add the tomatoes to the boiling water and leave on a high heat for 10 seconds (although this depends on how ripe the tomatoes are). Remove the tomatoes from the boiling water with a slotted spoon and plunge into a bowl of ice-cold water to refresh the tomato. Once cold, the tomatoes should peel easily. Cut into quarters and remove the seeds. The flesh of the tomato should still hold its structure. Cut into small even-sized dice and set aside.

Reuse the frying pan but reduce the heat to medium. Add the fish stock, lemon juice and cardamom seeds and reduce the liquid by half. Pass through a fine-mesh sieve into a small pot and return to the hob over a medium heat. Add the cream and the remaining butter. Bring the sauce almost to the boil, then reduce the heat and simmer for a further 2 minutes before adding the diced tomatoes and chives.

Remove the monkfish from the oven and cut into slices. Serve with the sauce spooned over.

salmon with roasted red peppers and parmesan

SERVES 4

2 red peppers

4 x 180g salmon fillets, skin on and deboned

salt and freshly ground black pepper

20g butter

juice of ½ lemon

40ml basil oil (page 164)

80g Parmesan cheese, grated

lemon cream sauce (page 102), to serve

new potatoes, to serve

This is an attractive fillet once baked, with the cheese melting around the peppers and basil.

Preheat the oven to 240°C.

Place the whole red peppers on a small baking tray and roast in the oven for 30 minutes, until the peppers are tender and dark. Place in a bowl, cover tightly with cling film and set aside to cool for 20 minutes. This allows the skin to crease further and makes it easy to peel. Carefully remove the core of the pepper by the stalk, then begin to peel by hand, ensuring all the seeds are removed. Finely dice the peppers.

Reduce the oven temperature to 180°C.

Season the salmon fillets on both sides with salt and pepper. Place a large frying pan over a medium heat. Add the butter and place the salmon in the pan, skin side down. Cook for 3 minutes, then carefully turn the salmon over and cook for a further 3 minutes. Squeeze the lemon juice into the pan, but not directly onto the fish. Remove the salmon from the pan and place on a baking tray.

Put a spoonful of the diced red pepper on the top of each of the fillets, drizzle with basil oil and sprinkle with cheese. Cook in the oven for 8 minutes, until the fish is very slightly undercooked, with a little give, and the cheese on top has melted through the peppers.

Serve with the lemon cream sauce and new potatoes.

GET AHEAD

The salmon can be prepared in advance, ready to go into the oven.

summer seabass with new potatoes, asparagus and vinaigrette

SERVES 4

12 asparagus spears

4 x 180g seabass fillets, skin on and deboned

salt and freshly ground black pepper

20g butter

4 cooked new potatoes, sliced

100g baby spinach leaves

FOR THE VINAIGRETTE:

1 red pepper

80ml olive oil

20ml white wine vinegar

juice of 1 lemon

zest of 1 lime

1 tsp caster sugar

1 tsp chopped chives

The idea of this particular dish is that it's quite easy to prepare. By roasting the fish fillets in the oven, you'll get a crisp skin on the seabass and you can concentrate on the other elements that you serve with it, which can change depending on availability and seasonality of ingredients. Courgettes and tomatoes also complement seabass.

Preheat the oven to 240°C.

To make the vinaigrette, place the whole red pepper on a small baking tray and roast in the oven for 30 minutes, until the pepper is tender and dark. Place in a bowl, cover tightly with cling film and set aside to cool for 20 minutes. This allows the skin to crease further and makes it easy to peel. Carefully remove the core of the pepper by the stalk, then begin to peel by hand, ensuring all the seeds are removed. Cut into even-sized dice.

When the pepper comes out of the oven, reduce the temperature to 190°C. Lightly brush a baking tray with oil.

Combine the olive oil, vinegar, lemon juice, lime zest and sugar in a small bowl. Add the diced roasted red pepper and chopped chives and set aside until required.

To prepare the asparagus, snap the tough ends off the spears (approx. 4–5cm off the ends), then carefully peel the ends of the stalk without removing too much actual asparagus. Cook the asparagus in a large saucepan of boiling salted water for approximately 2 minutes. There should still be a bit of bite in the asparagus (al dente).

Season the seabass fillets on both sides and place on the oiled baking tray. Cook in the oven for 8 minutes, until it's firm and cooked all the way through.

Melt the butter in a large frying pan set over a medium heat. Sauté the sliced cooked new potatoes for 3 minutes on each side, then add the asparagus and cook for 2 minutes. Add the spinach and stir until it has wilted, which will take approximately 30 seconds.

Put a spoonful of the potato, asparagus and spinach onto a warmed plate and place a seabass fillet of on top. Give the vinaigrette dressing a quick mix, then spoon 2 tablespoons of the dressing over the fish.

GET AHEAD

The vinaigrette dressing will keep in an airtight container in the fridge for over a week.

beef hotpot with horseradish mash

This is a hearty autumnal comfort dish.

Preheat the oven to 150°C.

Heat the oil in large ovenproof casserole over a medium heat. Brown the meat in small batches and set aside. Add the onions, carrots and celery and cook until softened and lightly browned. Lower the heat and return the meat and its juices to the casserole, then stir in the flour. Add the stock, garlic, thyme, rosemary, bay leaves and seasoning. Bring to a simmer, then cover with a lid and transfer to the oven to cook for 3–3½ hours, until the meat is tender. Taste to check if the stew requires additional seasoning.

To make the mash, boil the peeled and sliced potatoes in salted water until they are cooked through, then drain well. Warm the cream in a pot on the hob or in the microwave. Mash the potatoes, adding the butter and cream a little at a time, allowing the potatoes to soak in the liquid. Add the parsley and horseradish and continue mashing until the potatoes are creamy.

To serve, ladle the beef stew into warmed shallow bowls and top with the mash.

GET AHEAD

This hotpot can be made the day before if required.

SERVES 4–6

2 tbsp olive oil

1.5kg stewing beef

5 medium onions, sliced

2 carrots, cut into even-sized pieces

2 celery sticks, chopped

100g gluten-free plain white flour blend

500ml beef or chicken stock (page 148)

3 garlic cloves, crushed

3 sprigs of thyme

3 sprigs of rosemary

3 bay leaves

salt and freshly ground black pepper

FOR THE HORSERADISH MASH:

800g floury potatoes, such as Maris Piper or new season varieties, peeled and evenly sliced

110ml cream

120g butter

20g fresh flat-leaf parsley, chopped

10g fresh horseradish, grated, or 1 tbsp horseradish sauce

traditional roast rib of beef with yorkshire pudding

SERVES 4–6

2kg rib of beef, on the bone

4 carrots, roughly chopped

3 celery sticks, roughly chopped

2 onions, roughly chopped

sprig of thyme, chopped

sprig of rosemary, chopped

30ml olive oil

salt and freshly ground black pepper

50ml water

800ml beef stock

FOR THE YORKSHIRE PUDDING:

160g gluten-free plain white flour blend

20g cornflour

1 tsp xanthan gum

2 eggs

2 egg yolks

550ml milk

15g fresh thyme and rosemary, leaves picked and chopped

approx. 100ml vegetable oil

This particular cut of beef is one of the most flavoursome. It's a feast for meat lovers and well worth the effort. It does have more fat than a sirloin, but either cut is suitable.

Take the beef out of the fridge 1 hour before you intend to cook it so that it can come back up to room temperature.

Preheat the oven to 220°C.

Place the prepared vegetables in a large roasting tin. Score the beef fat with a sharp knife. Combine the chopped fresh herbs, olive oil, salt and pepper in a small bowl, then rub the beef all over with this mixture.

Place the beef on top of the vegetables in the roasting tin. Add the water to the tin to stop the vegetables from burning straight away, as the beef is initially cooking at quite a high temperature. Roast in the oven for 20 minutes, then reduce the temperature to 175°C for a further 60 minutes. Once the beef is cooked, the fat should be crisp and golden brown and firm to the touch.

Remove the beef from the oven, cover loosely with tin foil to keep it warm and allow it to rest for 20 minutes. This will help retain the juices in the meat before it's cut, which will make it more tender to eat. Once the beef comes out of the oven, raise the temperature to 200°C.

While the beef is roasting, you can prepare the batter for the Yorkshire pudding (or even better, make it the night before). Sieve the flour, cornflour and xanthan gum into a large bowl and make a well in the centre. Whisk the eggs and egg yolks together in a bowl, then add the egg to the flour and gradually add the milk, whisking to incorporate all the ingredients together. If at this point you think it may be a little lumpy, pass the batter through a fine-mesh sieve.

Add the chopped fresh herbs and season with salt and pepper. The batter should be a smooth pouring consistency.

Prepare the bun tin by putting a dessertspoon of oil into each cup of the tin and preheating the tin in the oven. Once the oil is hot, remove the tin from the oven, fill each cup halfway full with batter and bake for 15 minutes. After this time the Yorkshire puddings may look cooked, but they will need further cooking to ensure they hold their shape and don't collapse, so reduce the temperature to 160°C and cook for a further 10 minutes.

Remove the beef from the roasting tray and place on a dish. To make a jus, skim as much fat from the roasting pan as possible. Place the roasting tin on top of the hob and add 800ml stock or water to the tin. Stir the pan, scraping up any of the sediment stuck to the pan, including any vegetables. Bring to the boil, then pour the liquid through a fine-mesh sieve into a small saucepan. This liquid can be used for making the pepper cream sauce on page 154, or else you can just reduce this liquid by half, season and serve with the roast beef.

GET AHEAD

The batter for the Yorkshire pudding can be made the day before.

shepherd's pie

SERVES 4

12 Rooster potatoes

handful of rock salt, for baking the potatoes

100g butter

10 sprigs of fresh thyme, leaves picked and chopped

salt and freshly ground black pepper

75ml olive oil

230g onions, finely chopped

150g carrots, finely diced

800g minced lamb

400ml lamb or chicken stock (page 148)

200g peas

braised carrots with tarragon (page 144), to serve

The key to a good shepherd's pie is good-quality lamb mince, which you can get from your local butcher.

Preheat the oven to 200°C.

To prepare the baked potatoes, scrub the unpeeled potatoes well, then pat them dry. Prick the skin of the potatoes with a fork, then place on a baking tray with a handful of rock salt on the bottom – this soaks up the moisture in the potatoes while baking. Place in the oven and bake for 1¼ hours. When they're cool enough to handle, spoon the baked potatoes out of their jackets and mash with the butter, chopped fresh thyme, salt and pepper.

Meanwhile, heat the oil in a heavy-based saucepan over a medium heat. Add the onions and carrots and sweat for 3 minutes. Add the minced lamb and cook for about 5 minutes, until the mince has softened and separated. Season with salt and pepper.

Heat the stock in a separate saucepan, then add it to the lamb. Simmer for 10 minutes, adding the peas at the end. Allow to cool slightly.

Fill a 32cm x 26cm roasting tin or casserole dish with the minced lamb. Spoon the mashed potato on top of the lamb and cook in the oven for 25 minutes, until the potato has a nice crispy finish and is golden brown colour. Serve with braised carrots with tarragon.

the ultimate burger

SERVES 4

FOR THE BEEF BURGERS:

450g lean minced beef

2 small onions, finely chopped

2 garlic cloves, crushed

2 egg yolks

1 tsp paprika

1 tsp Dijon mustard

1 tsp gluten-free Worcestershire sauce

8 drops of Tabasco sauce

½ tsp salt

½ tsp cracked black pepper

10ml olive oil

4 slices of mozzarella

2 dessertspoons red onion marmalade (page 162)

2 dessertspoons homemade tomato ketchup (page 156)

FOR THE BUNS:

750g gluten-free white bread flour blend, plus extra for dusting

2 tsp salt

1½ tsp xanthan gum

40g fresh yeast or 2 tsp fast action dried yeast

50g butter, softened

425ml water

25ml milk

1 dessertspoon caster sugar

When the Fleadh Cheoil na hÉireann was held in Cavan a number of years ago, I set up a burger bar, which was a great success. It was one food item that I really missed and had to do a lot of homework on after I was diagnosed as being a coeliac. The burger bun is not a soft bun, but rather has a great crust that works well with the burger.

To make the buns, sieve the flour, salt and xanthan gum into the bowl of a stand mixer. If using dried yeast, add it at this point too. Add the softened butter and use the dough hook attachment to combine all the ingredients.

Mix the fresh yeast (if using), water, milk and caster sugar together to blend the yeast. Add to the dry ingredients and mix with the dough hook for 8–10 minutes. The dough should be wet and sticky. Leave the dough in the bowl, cover it with cling film and put in a warm place for at least 1 hour. It will increase in size.

Dust a baking tray and the worktop with flour. Transfer the dough onto the lightly floured worktop. Cut into 8 equal portions and shape into rounds (or if you want to make slider buns, shape them into smaller rounds). If the dough is too sticky when you are forming the buns, rub some olive oil on your hands. This will prevent the dough from sticking to your hands. Put on the prepared tray, dust with a little flour and leave to prove for 30 minutes. The dough will rise again.

Meanwhile, preheat the oven to 200°C. When the buns have risen again, bake them for 20–25 minutes, until they are crusty on top. To check that the buns are done, turn them over and tap the base. If you hear a light, hollow sound, the buns are ready for serving.

Reduce the oven temperature to 180°C.

Place the minced beef, onions, garlic, egg yolks, paprika, mustard, Worcestershire, Tabasco, salt and pepper in a large bowl and mix together well by hand. Divide the mixture into four even portions, then press and shape into burgers.

Heat the olive oil in a large heavy-based frying pan over a medium heat. Add the burgers to the pan and cook for 3 minutes on each side. Once the burgers are well sealed, place them on a baking tray and cook in the oven for 5 minutes to ensure they are cooked all the way through. Before removing from the oven, place a slice of mozzarella onto each burger, then return them to the oven or under a hot grill for 1 minute, just until the cheese begins to melt. Remove from the oven and toast the burger buns.

To assemble, put a spoonful of red onion marmalade on the bun, followed by the burger and cheese. Top with ketchup and finish with the other half of the bun. It may need to be held together with a cocktail stick.

GET AHEAD

You'll make eight burger buns but you only need four for these burgers. The leftover buns can be frozen after they are baked and thawed when required.

gluten-free pizza dough

MAKES 2 X 20CM PIZZAS

250g gluten-free bread flour, plus extra
for dusting

1 tsp xanthan gum

½ tsp salt

50g fresh yeast or 2¼ tsp fast action
dried yeast

150ml water

30ml olive oil

1 dessertspoon caster sugar

tomato sauce (page 158)

*There is nothing difficult about making this pizza dough. Don't be
afraid of using yeast. Once you follow the steps, you will be delighted
with yourself. Use any variations you wish as your toppings.*

Sieve together the flour, xanthan gum and salt in the bowl of a stand
mixer. If using dried yeast, add it at this point too. Use the dough
hook attachment to combine all the ingredients.

Add the fresh yeast (if using) to the water, olive oil and caster sugar
and mix well. The yeast will be absorbed into the liquid and it will
become cloudy. Add to the dry ingredients and mix with the dough
hook for 10 minutes. Leave the dough in the bowl, cover with cling
film and put in a warm place for 20 minutes to allow the yeast to
work.

Divide the dough equally into two pieces. Leave to rest for 10
minutes covered with a tea towel in a warm place. Lightly dust a
baking tray with flour.

Using a rolling pin, roll out each half of the dough until it's 20cm in
diameter. Place onto the floured baking tray and spoon the tomato
sauce all over the pizza base, leaving a 1cm rim clear around the edge.
Cover with your chosen toppings and leave to rest for 20 minutes.

Preheat the oven to 220°C. When it's ready, bake the pizza for
8 minutes.

GET AHEAD

*This dough can be made the day before, but it's important to line a baking tray with non-
stick baking paper brushed with oil. The dough can then be portioned and placed on the
tray and covered with another layer of non-stick baking paper brushed with oil, followed
by cling film, which will stop a skin from forming. Refrigerate overnight and remove from
the fridge 20 minutes before required.*

gluten-free pasta dough

SERVES 8

150g gluten-free rice flour

50g gluten-free cornmeal

3 large eggs

2 tbsp xanthan gum

1 tbsp cornflour

1 tbsp extra virgin olive oil

pinch of fine sea salt

gluten-free plain white flour blend, for dusting

If you want to go to the trouble of making fresh pasta, perhaps for a favourite pasta dish, a special occasion or a dinner party, then this recipe is very straightforward. It will take a little bit of labour if you don't have a pasta machine, but you will be pleased with the end result.

Place all the ingredients in a food processor and blitz to a rough dough. Dust your worktop with the plain flour. Tip the dough out onto the dusted surface and knead for 3–5 minutes, until smooth. Wrap the dough in cling film and leave to rest in the fridge for 30 minutes.

Cut the dough into four pieces, then carefully roll out each portion with a rolling pin until it's 1cm thick. At this point, roll it out using a pasta machine. (If you don't have a pasta machine, roll the dough with a rolling pin as thinly as possible, flouring the work surface as you go.) Start with the widest setting and feed the dough through the machine. Move the setting on the pasta machine down a notch and feed the dough through again. Continue with this process until the dough is at the required thickness, which is usually the second-last setting on the pasta machine. At this point the pasta dough can be cut into whatever shape you require, or change the setting on the pasta machine and run it through again for spaghetti, etc. Cover the pasta with a damp tea towel to prevent it from drying out.

The pasta is now ready to cook in boiling salted water. It should take 4–5 minutes to cook, depending on the thickness of the pasta.

GET AHEAD

Covered and stored in the fridge, this dough will last for up to a week.

children's favourites

WITH AWARENESS at an all-time high, more and more children are being diagnosed with coeliac disease. It can be difficult at the best of times to get kids to eat well, and if they're fussy eaters, it can be a downright nightmare. It's easy to fall into set food options for convenience and ease, but with children, especially if they have a food intolerance, it's important that they are introduced to a varied diet, good eating habits and food that is tasty and delicious. The following recipes are children's favourites. The children themselves can get involved in the preparation, which in turn will interest them more in eating well.

cheese croquettes

SERVES 4

500g potatoes, peeled and cut into pieces

1 tbsp olive oil

salt and freshly ground black pepper

75g mozzarella or Cheddar cheese, cut into 4cm x 1cm pieces

50g gluten-free plain white flour blend

3 eggs, beaten

100g gluten-free breadcrumbs

2 tsp dried chilli flakes (optional)

2 litres sunflower oil, for deep-frying

homemade tomato ketchup (page 156), to serve

When it comes to children's parties, these croquettes are a safe and popular choice, plus the children themselves love to get their hands messy making them. Mozzarella works best in the centre as it has a better melting quality, but Cheddar is good too. If the kids' taste buds are up to it, you could also add some chilli flakes to the breadcrumb coating.

Put the potatoes into a pan of lightly salted water and bring to the boil. Cook for about 15 minutes, until the potatoes are tender, then drain and return to the pan. Place the pan back over the heat for a few minutes to dry off any excess moisture from the potatoes, then remove from the heat and mash the potatoes until smooth. Beat in the olive oil, then season with salt and pepper and allow to cool. Once the potatoes are cool, break off a portion and mould it around the pieces of cheese into an oblong cylinder.

Place the flour in a shallow dish and the beaten eggs in a second shallow dish. Place the breadcrumbs and chilli flakes, if using, in a third shallow dish and mix them together.

Lightly flour each of the croquettes, then dip into the beaten eggs, shaking off any excess, followed by the breadcrumbs, making sure you evenly coat each of the croquettes. You may need to shape them further using a palette knife. Cover and refrigerate the croquettes for at least 20 minutes before cooking.

Heat the oil in a deep-fat fryer until it reaches 170°C (or you can shallow fry the croquettes in a frying pan). Fry the croquettes until they are crisp and golden. Once cooked, remove with a slotted spoon onto kitchen paper. These are great served with homemade tomato ketchup.

bangers and mash with onion gravy

SERVES 4

2kg potatoes, peeled and cut into chunks

100g butter

150ml cream

100ml milk

salt and freshly ground black pepper

4–8 gluten-free sausages (depending on size)

2 garlic cloves, sliced

1 bunch of fresh sage, leaves picked

1 bunch of fresh rosemary

1 tbsp olive oil

onion gravy (page 152)

This is comfort food at its best. There is more variety now in supermarkets and at your local butcher for gluten-free sausages. I advise trying many of them until you find the one that you like best. The ones with the most meat content are the tastiest and have less seasoning. In this recipe, the garlic, sage and rosemary enhance the flavour.

Preheat the oven to 190°C.

Place the potatoes in a pot of lightly salted water, bring to the boil and cook for 18–20 minutes, until tender and cooked through. Drain well and place the pot back on to the heat to dry out any excess water. Add the butter, cream, milk and seasoning and mash well. Cover with a piece of parchment paper to keep warm and set aside.

Meanwhile, place the sausages in a roasting tin with the garlic, sage and rosemary and drizzle with the olive oil. Bake for 7 minutes, then reduce the heat to 170°C, turn the sausages over in the tray and cook for a further 7 minutes, until the sausages are cooked all the way through with a golden, crisp finish.

Put a large spoonful of the creamy mashed potatoes on a warmed plate. Place one or two sausages on top and serve with plenty of onion gravy.

chicken and butter bean sliders

When you're trying to steer away from processed foods, especially for children, these burgers are a real winner. They're simple to make, with only a few basic ingredients.

SERVES 4

350g boneless, skinless chicken breasts

200g canned butter beans (no salt or sugar), drained, or home-cooked dried beans

1 medium onion, roughly chopped

1 garlic clove, peeled

50g gluten-free plain white flour blend, for shaping

4 gluten-free burger buns (page 117)

salad leaves, to serve

tomatoes, to serve

FOR THE PICKLED RED ONION:

1 red onion, thinly sliced

50g caster sugar

100ml white wine vinegar

To prepare the pickled red onion, place the onion, sugar and vinegar in a bowl, cover with cling film and pickle overnight in the refrigerator. Drain the excess liquid before serving with the burgers.

Place the chicken, butter beans, onion and garlic in a food processor and pulse until blended. Shape into small rounds with wet or floured hands.

Preheat the grill to high. Cook the burgers for 8 minutes, turning once or twice, until they are browned and cooked through. Alternatively, heat a non-stick frying pan over a medium heat, cook the burgers for about 4 minutes on each side and finish cooking in a 175°C oven for about 10 minutes. Once cooked, the burgers should have a golden brown finish and the juices must run clear.

Serve in a gluten-free burger bun with some lettuce, tomato and pickled red onions.

GET AHEAD

Wrap each uncooked burger with cling film after shaping into rounds if you want to freeze them.

sticky chicken wings

SERVES 4

3 garlic cloves, crushed

2 tbsp homemade tomato ketchup (page 156)

2 tbsp gluten-free soya sauce

1 tbsp soft brown sugar

4–6 drops of Tabasco (optional)

700g chicken wings, winglets removed

1 dessertspoon sesame seeds

seasonal salad, to serve

coleslaw, to serve

This is simply messy food that children love. Sorry!

Preheat the oven to 180°C.

Mix the garlic, tomato ketchup, soya sauce, brown sugar and Tabasco, if using, together in a large bowl. Add the chicken wings and mix well, coating all of the wings in the sauce. It can be left covered in the fridge to marinate for 30 minutes, otherwise pour out the chicken wings onto a large baking tray and roast in the oven for 30 minutes.

After 30 minutes, give the wings a stir and sprinkle with the sesame seeds. The chicken wings should be cooked all the way through and have a sticky finish. Serve with a seasonal salad and coleslaw.

chicken goujons with homemade tomato ketchup

SERVES 4–6

2 tbsp vegetable, sunflower or rapeseed oil

50g gluten-free plain white flour blend

3 medium eggs, beaten

150g gluten-free breadcrumbs, without the crusts

½ tsp cayenne pepper (optional)

salt and freshly ground black pepper

4 boneless, skinless chicken breasts, cut into even-sized strips

homemade tomato ketchup (page 156), to serve

fries, to serve

salad, to serve

This recipe is quite handy for children's parties, as the chicken can be prepared in advance. As the goujons are baked in the oven, it also cuts out a lot of mess during the party.

Preheat the oven to 190°C.

Drizzle 1 tablespoon of oil over two large baking trays and place them in the oven.

Place the flour in a shallow dish. Place the beaten eggs in a second shallow dish. Mix the breadcrumbs, cayenne pepper (if using) and some salt and pepper in a third shallow dish.

Dip the chicken pieces first in the plain flour, then into the beaten egg and finally coat in the breadcrumbs, shaking off the excess at each stage. Remove the trays from the oven and lay the goujons on the hot trays. Drizzle the goujons all over with the remaining tablespoon of oil.

Bake for 20 minutes, turning once. Remove from the oven when completely cooked through – cut one in the centre to make sure there is no pink. The coating should be golden brown all over.

Serve the chicken goujons with homemade ketchup and fries or salad.

GET AHEAD

To prepare the chicken in advance, place the uncooked breaded chicken on a cold tray, cover with cling film and refrigerate until required.

lemon sole goujons

SERVES 4

2 litres sunflower oil, for deep-frying

4 lemon sole fillets, skinned (ask your fishmonger to do this for you)

200g gluten-free plain white flour blend

salt and freshly ground black pepper

3 eggs, beaten

300g gluten-free breadcrumbs, without the crust

zest of 1 lemon

tartare sauce (page 167) or homemade ketchup (page 158), to serve

Children just love finger food and putting a light crumb on the fish keeps it moist during cooking. When preparing the breadcrumbs, try not to use the crust, as you will get a lighter, finer crumb finish. Any white fish can be used for this recipe, but I really like lemon sole as it's so delicate.

Heat the oil in a deep-fat fryer to 180°C.

Cut each lemon sole fillet into five or six even-sized strips, depending on the size of the fillets.

Place the flour in a shallow dish and season with salt and pepper. Place the beaten eggs in a second shallow dish. Mix the breadcrumbs and lemon zest together in a third shallow dish.

Dip the fish pieces first in the seasoned flour, then into the beaten egg and finally coat in the breadcrumbs, shaking off the excess at each stage. Place on a plate once the pieces are coated.

Carefully place in the deep-fat fryer and cook for 2–3 minutes. Serve with homemade tartare sauce or tomato ketchup.

mozzarella meatballs

SERVES 4

250g lean minced beef

1 small onion, finely chopped

1 egg, beaten

1 tsp chopped fresh parsley

freshly ground black pepper

½ ball of buffalo mozzarella, cut into 2cm cubes

gluten-free flour, for coating

3 tbsp olive oil

FOR THE SAUCE:

1 tsp olive oil

½ onion, finely chopped

1 celery stick, finely chopped

1 garlic clove, crushed

5 tomatoes, cut into quarters, seeds removed and chopped

1 tsp tomato purée

1 tsp light brown sugar

freshly ground black pepper

gluten-free pasta, to serve

freshly grated Parmesan cheese, to serve

This is a twist on meatballs for children, who love the gooey centre.

To make the meatballs, put the beef, onion, beaten egg and parsley in a bowl and mix well, adding pepper to taste. Mould the meat mixture around each cube of mozzarella, then roll the meatballs in the flour to coat. Heat the olive oil in a frying pan over a medium heat. Fry the meatballs for 10 minutes, until cooked through and browned.

To make the sauce, heat the olive oil in a saucepan over a low heat. Add the onion, celery and garlic and cook gently for 6 minutes, until soft. Add the chopped tomatoes, tomato purée, brown sugar and pepper to taste and cook for 6 minutes more.

Blitz the sauce with a hand-held blender, then pour it over the meatballs. Serve with gluten-free pasta and freshly grated Parmesan cheese.

GET AHEAD

Both the sauce and the meatballs can be made in advance.

spaghetti bolognese

SERVES 4

2 tbsp olive oil

80g onions, finely chopped

400g lean minced beef

3 garlic cloves, crushed

1 x 400g tin of chopped tomatoes

300ml beef stock

10g mixed fresh herbs, chopped, such as basil and flat-leaf parsley

salt and freshly ground black pepper

800g gluten-free spaghetti

80g butter

80g Parmesan cheese, grated

20g fresh flat-leaf parsley, chopped

An old reliable that never disappoints. This particular recipe is quite straightforward, and very little bits = very little giving out.

Heat the oil in a large heavy-based saucepan over a low heat. Sweat the onions until tender, but do not colour them. Add the minced beef and garlic to the onions. Cook until the beef has browned and has broken into pieces, then add the tomatoes, stock and herbs. Bring to the boil, then reduce the heat, season lightly with salt and pepper and simmer for 40 minutes.

Meanwhile, bring a large pot of water to the boil with a pinch of salt. Cook the pasta according to the packet instructions, until al dente. Drain in a colander and lightly refresh by running some cold water through the cooked spaghetti.

Melt the butter in a shallow saucepan. Add the cooked spaghetti, season well and stir until thoroughly reheated.

Place the spaghetti in individual serving dishes with the hot Bolognese sauce spooned on top. Sprinkle with Parmesan cheese and garnish with the chopped parsley.

sides, stocks and sauces

THIS IS AN AREA where many coeliacs can get caught out, as most stocks and sauces contain gluten. Having perfected plenty of recipes, I really don't see the need for any of these to be flour based, as most work so well without it.

spiced lentils

SERVES 4

200g Puy lentils

1 tbsp olive oil

5 shallots, chopped

5 garlic cloves, chopped

1 green chilli, deseeded and chopped

25g root ginger, peeled and chopped

3 sprigs of thyme

3 sprigs of rosemary

500ml chicken stock (page 148)

1 tbsp caster sugar

Lentils are so versatile. They go well with any fish, poultry or meat and are a welcome change from potatoes.

Soak the lentils overnight in cold water or for 2 hours before cooking. Once soaked, place the lentils in a sieve and rinse well with running water.

Heat the olive oil in a large saucepan and sauté the shallots, garlic, chilli and ginger for 3 minutes. Pour in the lentils along with the thyme and rosemary and enough stock to cover and mix well.

Simmer gently for 1 hour, adding more stock if required. If the liquid evaporates too quickly, the lentils won't cook. Add the sugar and season to taste. Reheat as necessary before serving.

caramelised shallots

SERVES 4

2 tbsp olive oil

16 shallots, peeled and left whole

35g butter

35g caster, brown or Demerara sugar

100ml chicken stock (page 146)

salt and freshly ground black pepper

These are a smarter version of fried onions and are a delicious accompaniment to most meat dishes or sauces. The final dish should be beautifully tender shallots with a rich buttery and caramel flavour. Caramelised shallots are the ideal accompaniment to steak.

Heat the olive oil in a large frying pan over a medium heat. Add the shallots, butter and sugar. Cook gently for 10–15 minutes, until the sugar starts to caramelise and change colour. The shallots will take on a rich, golden colour. Gradually add the chicken stock, allowing each addition to become absorbed before adding more. Season with salt and pepper.

red cabbage and apple

SERVES 4

1 head of red cabbage, finely shredded

4 shallots, finely chopped

3 firm eating apples, cored and sliced

2 garlic cloves, chopped

2 sprigs of thyme

3 tbsp brown sugar (Demerara or any type of brown sugar)

2 tbsp water

60g butter

6 tbsp cider vinegar

salt and freshly ground black pepper

Cooking red cabbage can be as complicated as you like, but I choose to prepare a more simplified version. This vegetable is a great accompaniment to rich meat or game dishes. When shredding the red cabbage, either use a food processor or wear disposable gloves so that it doesn't stain your hands.

Put all the ingredients except for the butter and cider vinegar into a large saucepan. Cover with a lid and simmer for 1 hour.

Stir in the butter and cider vinegar and season with salt and pepper. Cover and cook for a further 10 minutes, until the cabbage is tender.

braised carrots with tarragon

SERVES 4

35g butter

15 baby carrots or new season carrots, peeled

30ml chicken stock (page 148)

salt and white pepper

10g fresh tarragon, chopped

The addition of fresh tarragon to these carrots is a classic combination that simply works. It adds a fresh new dimension to the carrots.

Preheat the oven to 175°C.

Melt the butter in a medium saucepan over a medium heat. Sweat the carrots for 5 minutes, then add the chicken stock and transfer to an ovenproof dish. Season lightly and cook in the oven for 10–15 minutes. The carrots should be tender and cooked all the way through, with a glossy sheen from the butter. To serve, toss in the fresh chopped tarragon.

fondant potatoes

4 potatoes, each weighing
about 300g peeled

3 tbsp vegetable oil

600ml chicken stock (page 148)

3 garlic cloves, crushed

2 sprigs of rosemary

80g butter, cubed, at room temperature

salt

This is a different twist on a roast potato that's a little more of a challenge – it's classical cooking, really.

Preheat the oven to 175°C.

Cut the potatoes into 4cm or 5cm squares that are 3cm thick. Heat the oil in a small roasting tin on top of the hob over a medium heat. Put the potatoes into the pan and brown lightly on all sides. Pour the stock into the pan and add the garlic and rosemary. Add the cubed butter and season with salt.

Put the roasting tin into the oven and cook for 30 minutes, until the liquid has evaporated and the potatoes are tender. To check if they are fully cooked, test them with a knife – there should be no resistance. While they are cooking, spoon the liquid over the potatoes to glaze them and give them a golden colour.

gratin potato

SERVES 4

10g butter

6 medium potatoes, peeled

salt and white pepper

220ml cream

3 garlic cloves, crushed

A luxurious potato dish that you can't help but eat more and more of.

Preheat the oven to 170°C. Grease the inside of an ovenproof, ceramic or roasting tin (ideally 20cm x 30cm x 3cm) with the butter.

Slice the peeled potatoes as thinly as possible. If you're lucky enough to have a mandolin, you can use this, slicing the potatoes no thicker than 0.5cm. Do not rinse the potatoes, as you will remove the starch that is required to make the finished gratin richer. Neatly layer the potatoes in the dish, lightly seasoning each layer.

Mix the cream and garlic together with a little seasoning, then pour it over the potatoes. The potatoes should be completely covered – if not, add more cream.

Bake the potatoes in the oven for 1½ hours, until they are soft, thick and creamy. The top of the baked gratin potato should a golden brown colour. The cooking time may vary slightly, depending on the variety of potato used.

GET AHEAD

I have often used cooked peeled potatoes to make this potato dish, which reduces the cooking time significantly.

chicken stock

MAKES 2 LITRES

1.5kg chicken bones or wings

1 large onion, chopped

1 leek, chopped

3 celery sticks, chopped

4 garlic cloves, peeled

2 bay leaves

sprig of thyme

sprig of rosemary

Of all the stocks, this is the easiest to make in terms of sourcing the ingredients. There is a noticeable difference between a commercial and a homemade stock.

Place the chicken bones or wings into a large saucepan and cover with water. Bring to the boil, then reduce the heat and simmer for 30 minutes. Skim to remove any impurities or froth from the top.

Add the onion, leek, celery, garlic and herbs. Simmer gently for 2 hours, skimming as necessary. Remove from the heat and allow to cool for 30 minutes.

Pass the stock through a sieve into a bowl. Discard all the ingredients, retaining only the liquid. Use and store as required.

GET AHEAD

This stock can be kept refrigerated for up to three days. Alternatively, you can freeze this stock in batches and use as required.

fish stock

MAKES 2 LITRES

1.5kg white fish bones

10g butter

2 onions, chopped

3 celery sticks, chopped

1 fennel bulb, roughly chopped

1 leek, white part only, chopped

1 lemon, halved

5 sprigs of parsley

5 sprigs of coriander

2.5 litres cold water

Using a homemade fish stock adds an authentic flavour to any sauces or soups. I find turbot bones are the best when making fish stock. Use the large bones from the fish where possible.

Rinse the fish bones under cold water and set aside.

Melt the butter in a heavy-based pan over a low heat. Add the onions, celery, fennel and leek and sweat slowly for about 10 minutes, until soft.

Add the fish bones, lemon halves and coriander and parsley sprigs. Pour in the cold water and bring to the boil. Skim to remove any impurities or froth from the top. Lower the heat and simmer gently for 20 minutes, then remove from the heat and allow to cool. Pass the stock through a sieve into a bowl. Discard all the ingredients, retaining only the liquid. Use and store as required.

GET AHEAD

The stock will last for three days in the fridge. Alternatively, you can freeze this stock in batches and use as required.

béchamel sauce

MAKES 1.5 LITRES

1 onion, peeled and left whole

8 whole cloves

1 litre milk

sprig of thyme

100g butter

100g gluten-free plain white flour blend

pinch of grated nutmeg

pinch of salt

pinch of white pepper

When preparing béchamel sauce, boiling it gives body and stability to the sauce. This is especially important if the sauce is used as a base for any pie. Adding 200g of white Cheddar will make a rich cheese sauce suitable for cauliflower cheese or macaroni.

Stud the onion with the cloves, then place into a medium-sized pot with the milk and thyme and bring to the boil. Remove from the heat and set aside for 20 minutes. This allows the onion, cloves and thyme to infuse into the milk, enhancing its flavour. When the time is up, remove the onion and thyme and discard them.

Melt the butter in a heavy-based saucepan. Stir in the flour and cook for 1 minute to make a roux. Gradually add small quantities of the warm milk to the roux, stirring continuously. If you don't stir constantly or if the milk is added too quickly, the sauce will become very lumpy. When all the milk has been added, bring the sauce to the boil, stirring continuously, then remove from the heat. Stir in a pinch of grated nutmeg, salt and white pepper. Cover with buttered greaseproof paper with a small hole cut out on top to prevent a skin from forming on the sauce.

If you are not happy with the consistency, don't be afraid to add more milk to lighten the sauce if required.

hollandaise sauce

MAKES 200ML

125g butter, clarified

2 shallots, finely chopped

50ml white wine vinegar

3 egg yolks

50ml white wine

salt and white pepper

This is a really versatile sauce. It's wonderful with fish, eggs and steak.

To clarify the butter, melt it in a small pot over a medium heat, then remove from the heat and leave to cool slightly, which allows the clear melted butter to rise to the top and the white solids to settle at the bottom. Skim the pure butter from the top and set aside.

Using a medium-sized saucepan, cook the shallots in the white wine vinegar, reducing the liquid but taking care not to discolour the shallots.

Using a large, deep stainless steel or Pyrex glass bowl, add the cooked shallots and liquid, the egg yolks and the white wine and whisk together. Put the bowl over a pot of simmering water, taking care not to let the water touch the bottom of the bowl. Continuously whisk the egg yolk mixture until it's a light, airy foam.

When the yolks start to thicken, remove the bowl from the saucepan of water. Before adding the melted butter to the egg yolk mixture, ensure the egg yolks are not too hot or the mixture might curdle.

Gradually add the melted butter using a ladle. Continue whisking as you are adding the butter, allowing the butter to become well combined before adding more butter. Once all the butter has been added, taste and season if necessary.

GET AHEAD

If you prepare extra shallot and white wine vinegar reduction, it can be stored in the refrigerator and used as needed. If you want to make the sauce a little bit ahead of time, stir in 1 tablespoon of water at the end to help stabilise it.

béarnaise sauce

Stir in some chopped fresh tarragon at the end of the hollandaise.

onion gravy

SERVES 4–6

2 tbsp vegetable oil

2 large onions, thinly sliced

20g light brown sugar

200ml red wine

100ml beef or chicken stock (page 148)

salt and freshly ground black pepper

This sweet, moreish gravy works very well with most roasts and is delicious with creamed potatoes.

Heat the oil in a heavy-based saucepan over a low heat. Add the onions and cook very slowly for 30 minutes. Stir occasionally and check that the onions aren't burning. They will change colour to a golden brown.

Add the brown sugar, red wine and stock to the onions and allow to simmer for 20 minutes. This should reduce the liquid by half. Taste and season as required.

pepper cream

SERVES 4–6

100g red onion marmalade (page 162)

10g green peppercorns

3 tbsp brandy

150ml chicken stock (page 148)

150ml cream

salt

The perfect sauce to serve with roast beef or steak.

Place the red onion marmalade and green peppercorns in a small saucepan. Heat until warmed through, then add the brandy and cook until it has reduced by half and the alcohol has been cooked out, which ensures the sauce will not be bitter. Add the chicken stock and reduce by half. Finally, add the cream and cook a little further, until a sauce consistency is achieved. Taste and season as required.

bread sauce

SERVES 6

1 onion, peeled and left whole

8 cloves

800ml milk

250g gluten-free breadcrumbs

50g butter

salt and freshly ground black pepper

This sauce is ideal with chicken or duck.

Stud the onion with the cloves, then place into a medium-sized pot with the milk and bring to the boil. Remove from the heat and set aside for 20 minutes. This allows the onion and cloves to infuse into the milk, enhancing its flavour. Remove the onion from the milk and discard it, then stir in the breadcrumbs and butter and mix together well. Return the sauce to a low heat, taste and correct the seasoning. Serve immediately.

apple and calvados sauce

MAKES 150ML

50g butter, cubed

2 Granny Smith apples, peeled, cored and diced

30ml Calvados (apple brandy)

200ml good-quality chicken stock (page 148)

salt and freshly ground black pepper

This is a wonderful sauce to serve with any pork dishes. It's also the perfect accompaniment to the black and white pudding terrine on page 26.

Place a 1 litre saucepan over a medium heat, add about 10g of butter and let it melt. Add the diced apples and sauté for 2 minutes, then add the Calvados. Simmer until the apple brandy has reduced by half, keeping in mind that the Calvados may flame when burning off the alcohol. Add the chicken stock and bring to the boil, then gradually add the rest of the butter, stirring continuously for 2 minutes. Taste and season as required.

homemade tomato ketchup

MAKES 600ML

100g Demerara or caster sugar

300ml cider vinegar or white wine vinegar

1kg ripe tomatoes, quartered

100g tomato purée

20g gluten-free English mustard

10g sea salt

3 garlic cloves, crushed

3 bay leaves

2 cinnamon sticks

2 cloves

1 tsp ground coriander

dash of Tabasco

This homemade ketchup has the same texture and consistency of a shop-bought ketchup. It's easy to make, stores well in the fridge and doesn't contain any unnecessary preservatives.

Place the sugar and vinegar in a heavy-based saucepan and bring to a simmer. Add all the remaining ingredients and bring to the boil, stirring to prevent the mixture from sticking to the bottom of the saucepan. Once it reaches the boil, reduce the temperature to a simmer, stirring occasionally, for 45 minutes.

Remove the bay leaves, cinnamon sticks and cloves and blend the remaining mix in a food processor or liquidiser. Push the mixture through a fine-mesh sieve to produce a smooth consistency. Taste again to correct the seasoning and pour into a clean jar with a tight-fitting lid.

GET AHEAD

This ketchup will keep for up to three weeks in the refrigerator.

tomato sauce

MAKES 800ML

2 tbsp olive oil

1 onion, chopped

1 celery stick, chopped

1 leek, white part only, chopped

3 garlic cloves, chopped

5g root ginger, peeled and chopped

sprig of thyme

sprig of rosemary

100g light brown sugar

100ml red wine

30ml red wine vinegar

4 x 400g tins of chopped tomatoes

10g fresh basil leaves

salt and freshly ground black pepper

This rich tomato sauce works well with any pasta or as a pizza base.

Heat the olive oil in a large saucepan over a medium heat. Add the onion, celery, leek, garlic, ginger, thyme and rosemary and cook for 3 minutes without letting the vegetables colour. Add the sugar, red wine and red wine vinegar and cook for a further 3 minutes. Stir in the chopped tomatoes and reduce the heat to the lowest setting.

Cover the sauce with a disc of greaseproof paper and allow the sauce to cook slowly for 1 hour. When the sauce has reduced and thickened, add the fresh basil leaves. Remove the pan from the heat and allow to cool slightly, then use a hand-held blender to purée the sauce. Taste and season if required.

GET AHEAD

This sauce will keep for up two weeks in an airtight container in the fridge. However, it does not freeze well.

mayonnaise

MAKES 500ML

3 egg yolks, at room temperature

2 tsp white wine vinegar

2 tsp Dijon mustard

500ml vegetable oil

fine sea salt and ground white pepper

It's a great accomplishment to succeed at making your own mayonnaise. The difference in taste is immense.

Whisk the egg yolks with the white wine vinegar and Dijon mustard in a food processor at full speed for 1 minute. Turn the food processor to half speed and add the vegetable oil very slowly – it should take 2–3 minutes to fully incorporate the oil. The finished product should be creamy and rich. Season to taste with salt and pepper. Homemade mayonnaise will keep for up to one week in an airtight container in the fridge.

mango mayonnaise

Add 200ml of mango purée to the mayonnaise at the end. Mango mayonnaise works well with crab cakes (page 41), prawns in tempura (page 38) and red onion marmalade (page 162).

red onion marmalade

MAKES APPROX. 1KG

150g butter

2.5kg red onions, thinly sliced

6 garlic cloves

1 chilli, deseeded and chopped

2 tsp chopped fresh thyme

200g light brown sugar

500ml red wine

300ml red wine vinegar

300ml port

A great accompament to any salad, fish or meats.

Melt the butter in a large heavy-based saucepan over a low heat. Add the onions, garlic, chilli and thyme and slowly cook for 30 minutes. Add the sugar, red wine, vinegar and port. Bring to the boil, then reduce the heat to a simmer for 1½ hours, keeping an eye on it and stirring occasionally from time to time.

Spoon into clean glass jars or other airtight containers.

GET AHEAD

This red onioin marmalade will keep in the fridge for up to four weeks.

basil oil

MAKES 500ML

200g fresh basil leaves

500ml olive oil

2 garlic cloves, crushed

salt

A herb oil is a wonderful light dressing on its own over salad leaves or simply drizzled over bruschetta or chargrilled or roasted vegetables.

Bring a small pan of salted water to the boil. Plunge the basil into the water for 5 seconds, then remove the basil immediately and put into cold water. Once cooled, drain and squeeze it.

Put the basil into a blender with the olive oil, crushed garlic and some salt. Blend until it becomes green and the basil seems to have disappeared. Strain the herb oil through a fine-mesh sieve to remove any bits to give it a smooth finish. Pour the oil into a covered container.

GET AHEAD

Basil oil will keep in the fridge for up to two weeks.

honey mustard dressing

MAKES 150ML

1 garlic clove, crushed

3 tbsp honey

2 tbsp Dijon mustard

1 tbsp wholegrain mustard

1 tbsp balsamic vinegar

125ml sunflower or olive oil

salt and freshly ground black pepper

This is one of our house dressings at The Olde Post Inn. It is certainly tried and tested.

Put the garlic, honey, mustards and balsamic vinegar in a food processor and whizz to combine. With the motor still running, slowly pour in the oil, allowing the oil to combine with all the ingredients and emulsify. Using a spatula, remove the dressing from the food processor. Season with salt and pepper. Store in a sealed container.

GET AHEAD

This dressing will keep for up to two weeks in the fridge.

wild garlic pesto

MAKES 220ML

40g pine nuts

200g wild garlic leaves

80g Parmesan cheese, grated

200ml extra virgin olive oil

sea salt and freshly ground black pepper

There is an abundance of wild garlic available around April. It is easily identified by its pungent smell and it makes a wonderful pesto.

Toast the pine nuts in a dry frying pan until they are light brown, taking care not to let them burn. Leave to cool.

Blend the cooled pine nuts, wild garlic, Parmesan and extra virgin olive oil in a food processor to form a thick paste. Season with the sea salt and freshly ground black pepper. Taste and adjust if necessary.

GET AHEAD

Stored in a sealed container in the fridge, the pesto will keep for up to two weeks.

tartare sauce

300ml mayonnaise

15g capers, chopped

2 medium gherkins, chopped

2 hardboiled eggs, peeled and chopped

1 dessertspoon finely chopped fresh parsley

juice of ½ lemon

Place all the ingredients in a bowl and combine well. This shouldn't need any seasoning.

dessert

IF YOU HAVE a sweet tooth like I do, then the very thought of having to give up pastries or cakes will send a shiver down your spine. We have a fantastic pastry chef in The Olde Post Inn who I have worked with very closely over the years, perfecting recipes.

Many shop-bought desserts are filled with sugar and preservatives, so I make my own sweets, which are by far a much tastier and healthier alternative. We've had many occasions in the restaurant where a coeliac diner has had to double check that their dessert was indeed suitable for them, so we must be doing something right.

sweet shortcrust pastry

**MAKES ENOUGH FOR 1 X 20CM
FLAN TIN**

225g gluten-free plain white flour blend

50g icing sugar

1 tsp xanthan gum

150g cold butter, cubed

1 egg, beaten

This sweet shortcrust pastry can be used as a base for many recipes. This recipe is typical of any shortcrust pastry – it may appear a little wet when made and will need to rest for an hour before use.

Mix the flour, icing sugar and xanthan gum together in a large bowl. Rub in the cold butter with your fingertips until the mixture resembles fine breadcrumbs. It's important that the butter is cool and not at room temperature, as the pastry will be tough if the butter is soft.

Make a well in the centre of the pastry and add the beaten egg. Combine all of the ingredients by hand, but try to work quickly to prevent the pastry from becoming too greasy. This mixture can be quite wet when it's mixed, but once it's rested it's easy to use.

Once combined, form the dough into a ball, wrap in cling film and leave to rest for at least 1 hour in the fridge. (It's also worth resting the dough for 20–30 minutes in the fridge after you line a flan tin and before filling it to reduce the possibility of shrinkage.)

Remove the pastry from the fridge, roll it out on a lightly floured work surface and use it to line a 20cm flan tin. Prod the base of the pastry all over with a fork and return to the fridge for 20–30 minutes.

Preheat the oven to 175°C. Cover the pastry with a layer of non-stick baking paper, ensuring the paper drapes over the edge of the tin and that it's fitted snugly into the edges of the tin as well.

Fill with dried beans or ceramic beans. If you don't have dried beans or ceramic beans, you can add a layer of tin foil over the baking paper and push it tightly into the edges. Place in the oven and bake for 15 minutes. Remove the baking paper and the beans and bake for a further 10 minutes.

If you're using individual small pastry tins, line the tins with the pastry, prod the pastry and return to the fridge for 10 minutes. They can then be baked blind without the need for non-stick baking paper and beans.

GET AHEAD

The uncooked pastry will keep in the fridge for up to five days. Alternatively, wrap it very well in cling film and freeze for up to four weeks.

apple and pecan crumble tart

SERVES 8–10

1 batch of sweet shortcrust pastry
(page 170)

1kg cooking apples, peeled, cored and
quartered

250g caster sugar

FOR THE CRUMBLE TOPPING:

150g gluten-free plain flour

80g cold butter, cubed

60g caster sugar

60g Demerara brown sugar

50g pecans, roughly chopped

TO SERVE:

vanilla ice cream (page 204)

This is a real comfort dessert that I remember having as a child. You cannot beat the smell of it baking and then tucking into it. There are never any leftovers!

Make sure you allow the pastry to rest for at least 1 hour. Use it to line a 20cm flan tin and bake blind as per the instructions on page 170. Let the pastry cool slightly to make it easier to assemble the crumble.

Once the pastry comes out of the oven, raise the temperature to 180°C.

Cut the quartered apples into chunks and place in a saucepan with the caster sugar. Place the saucepan on a high heat and cook, stirring continuously, until the apples change colour slightly but still hold their shape. It's important to avoid overcooking the apples at this stage or the apples will lose their shape and structure and the pastry will become soggy. Set the cooked apples aside to cool.

To make the crumble topping, sieve the flour into a large bowl and rub in the cold cubed butter until the mixture resembles breadcrumbs. Add the caster sugar, Demerara brown sugar and pecans and mix well.

Place the cooked apples in the cooled pastry case. Top with the crumble mix, spreading it to the edges of the pastry case to ensure that the cooked apples are fully covered.

Bake in the oven for 20–25 minutes, until the topping is golden. Serve warm with a scoop of vanilla ice cream.

GET AHEAD

If you want to make elements of this in advance, then the crumble topping will keep in your fridge for one week in a sealed container. Once cooked and cooled, the apples can be frozen in batches or kept in the fridge for up to five days.

lemon meringue pie

SERVES 8 • FOR THE PASTRY:

225g gluten-free plain white flour blend

50g icing sugar

1 tsp xanthan gum

150g cold butter, cubed

1 egg, beaten

zest of 1 lemon

1 vanilla pod, cut in half and seeds scraped out

FOR THE LEMON CURD FILLING:

1 tbsp cornflour

125ml single cream

5 eggs

175g caster sugar

3 lemons, juice of 3 and zest of 2

FOR THE MERINGUE:

7 egg whites (200g)

300g caster sugar

This is an old-time classic dessert, loved by all. Making it as individual tartlets gives it the wow factor. This isn't a simple dessert, but it's worth the effort. The addition of the lemon zest to pastry gives it some extra zing.

Make the pastry as per the instructions on page 170, adding the lemon zest and vanilla seeds to the dry ingredients. Make sure you allow the pastry to rest for at least 1 hour. Use it to line a 20cm flan tin or 8 individual tartlet tins and bake blind as per the instructions on page 170. Raise the oven temperature to 180°C.

To make the filling, dissolve the cornflour in a cup with 1 tablespoon of the cream. Mix together the eggs, sugar, the remaining cream and the lemon zest and juice. Place in a saucepan and bring to the boil, stirring all the time. Reduce the heat and simmer for 2 minutes to ensure it's cooked, then pour the curd into the cooled pastry case. If using a 20cm flan tin, return it to the oven and bake for 5 minutes to ensure the curd sets. If making individual tarts, there's no need to do this.

To make the meringue, use the balloon whisk attachment on your mixer to whip the egg whites to soft peaks. Gradually add the caster sugar, whisking on a high speed until it's stiff and glossy. This should take about 10 minutes.

Cover the lemon curd with the meringue. You can either use a piping bag with a nozzle to pipe the meringue onto the curd or you could use a spoon and a palette knife, making peaks with the back of the spoon or knife.

Place the pie in the oven and bake for 8–10 minutes, until the meringue is light golden. Allow the pie to cool before cutting into slices.

rhubarb baked alaska

MAKES 5 • FOR THE RHUBARB COMPOTE:

450g rhubarb, cut into 0.5cm dice

150g caster sugar

juice of 1 lemon

FOR THE SPONGE:

3 eggs

90g caster sugar

70g gluten-free self-raising flour

20g cornflour

FOR THE MERINGUE:

3 large eggs whites (100g egg whites)

150g caster sugar

TO ASSEMBLE:

good-quality vanilla ice cream (page 204)

icing sugar, to dust

This dessert is truly delightful and perfect if you want to impress guests. The key to this recipe is to have all of the different elements ready, and then assembly is straightforward. This recipe makes more compote and sponge than you'll need, but as both can be frozen, you can save them for another day. You could also use these sponge discs instead of the amaretti biscuits in the tiramisu on page 196.

First prepare the rhubarb compote by mixing all of the compote ingredients together in a bowl. Cover with cling film and refrigerate overnight to allow the juices to run. The next day, bring the rhubarb mixture to the boil in a small saucepan, then reduce the heat and simmer for 2–3 minutes, taking care not to overcook the rhubarb as you want it to retain its shape. Pour into a container until required.

Scoop the ice cream into balls ahead of time and place on a sheet of non-stick baking paper. Put in a container and put them back in the freezer, ready for assembly.

Preheat the oven to 180°C. Line a large rectangular baking tin (ideally one that is 20cm x 30cm x 5cm deep) with non-stick baking paper.

To make the sponge, place the eggs and sugar in a mixing bowl and beat together with an electric mixer for about 10 minutes, until it reaches the ribbon stage and the mixture holds a figure of eight. Sieve the flour and cornflour into a separate bowl. Using a metal spoon, gently fold the dry ingredients into the egg mixture, ensuring they are well combined.

Carefully pour the sponge batter into the lined tin and bake for 25 minutes, until the sponge starts to shrink away from the sides of the tin and the centre springs back when you press it. Remove from the oven and leave to cool in the tin, then turn out onto a board and peel off the paper. Using a round 5cm cutter, stamp out your sponge discs – you should get 22 discs.

To make the meringue, whisk the egg whites in a spotlessly clean, grease-free bowl to the soft peak stage, until they are light and stiff. Gradually add the sugar, whisking continuously on a medium speed. Once all the sugar has been added, whisk at a high speed for about 2 minutes, until the meringue is glossy. Fill the meringue into a clean, dry piping bag with a nozzle and set aside.

To assemble the baked Alaska, place the sponge discs on a baking tray lined with non-stick baking paper. Spoon a little rhubarb compote over each sponge disc, ensuring it is well moistened with the rhubarb syrup. Put a scoop of vanilla ice cream on top, then pipe the meringue all over the ice cream and sponge, ensuring it's completely covered with meringue. Alternatively, you could use a spoon to cover the sponge with meringue, making peaks with the back of the spoon. Dust with icing sugar and bake for 1–2 minutes, until the meringue is set and slightly coloured. Serve immediately.

GET AHEAD

The sponge and the rhubarb can be prepared in advance – both freeze very well if you really want to get a good head start.

crème anglaise

MAKES 550ML

500ml single cream

1 vanilla pod

50g icing sugar

5 egg yolks

This is a very simple recipe, but it's important to follow it accurately and it's best made with good-quality egg yolks. Served warm, the custard is an ideal accompaniment for tarts or crumbles and it can be used cold in trifles.

Place the cream in a large heavy-based saucepan. It's important to use a large saucepan to allow the cream to rise and triple in size as it cooks.

Cut the vanilla pod in half and scrape the seeds out into the cream. Place the seedless vanilla pod into the saucepan too along with 25g of the icing sugar. Bring to the boil, stirring occasionally.

In a heatproof bowl, whisk the egg yolks and the remaining 25g of icing sugar until fully combined and smooth.

Pour the boiling cream into the egg mixture and whisk well. Pour the custard through a fine-mesh sieve back into the saucepan to remove the vanilla pod and any lumps. Return the mixture to a low heat, whisking continuously until the custard coats the back of a spoon.

NOTE: The number of egg yolks will vary according to size. As a guide, one egg yolk should weigh 20g to achieve a good egg custard consistency.

GET AHEAD

The custard can be served immediately or kept in the fridge for three days with a sheet of cling film pressed directly on the surface so that a skin doesn't form on it.

cherry clafoutis

MAKES 6 PORTIONS

butter, for greasing

caster sugar, for dusting

3 eggs

50g honey

150ml cream

150ml milk

1 tbsp kirsch

80g gluten-free plain white flour blend

1 x 425g tin of cherries

crème anglaise (page 179), to serve

vanilla ice cream (page 204), to serve

This is ideal if you are entertaining guests and want to serve a warm dessert straight from the oven that is both light and not too sweet.

Preheat the oven to 170°C. Grease six ramekins or shallow dishes (4.5cm x 5.5cm) with butter and dust with a little caster sugar, tapping out the excess sugar. Alternatively, you could use one large dish or pan.

Whisk together the eggs, honey, cream, milk and kirsch. Sieve the flour into a large mixing bowl, make a well in the centre and pour in the wet ingredients. Whisk into a smooth batter, then pour the batter through a fine-mesh sieve into a jug.

Drain the cherries and remove any stones. Divide them equally between the ramekins.

Before pouring the batter into the moulds, give it a good stir to make sure the flour is distributed. Cover the cherries with the batter. If using ramekins, only fill them three-quarters full to allow the mixture to rise. Place the ramekins on a baking tray and bake for 10–12 minutes. Once baked, the clafoutis will have increased in height, turned golden in colour, and when lightly pressed in the middle it will give but return to its shape.

Serve with crème anglaise and ice cream.

GET AHEAD

The batter can be made in advance and baked when required.

baked raspberry
cheesecake with raspberry jelly

SERVES 12 • FOR THE CHEESECAKE:

700g full-fat cream cheese

120g caster sugar

1 tsp vanilla essence or the seeds from
1 vanilla pod

3 large eggs

80g fresh or frozen raspberries

FOR THE BISCUIT BASE:

220g gluten-free biscuits

100g butter, melted

FOR THE JELLY:

3 leaves of gelatine or 2½ tsp powdered
gelatine

75g caster sugar

150ml water

150g fresh or frozen raspberries

1 dessertspoon crème de cassis, or to
taste

TO DECORATE:

fresh Chantilly cream

fresh raspberries

*The raspberries in this baked cheesecake are a pleasant variation and means
it's not too filling, which some baked cheesecakes can be.*

Line a 20cm springform cake tin with non-stick baking paper. Wrap
the outside of the base and sides of the cake tin with cling film, then
wrap again with tin foil. The cheesecake will be baked in a water
bath (bain-marie), so the cling film seals the tin and prevents the
water from spoiling the cheesecake as it bakes.

Whizz the biscuits into fine crumbs in a food processor or place them
in a sealed plastic bag and crush with a rolling pin. Add the melted
butter and mix well. Place the biscuit mixture into the prepared tin,
pressing it firmly into the base with the back of a spoon. Allow it to
set in the fridge for 20–30 minutes.

Preheat the oven to 170°C.

Using the balloon whisk attachment of your food mixer, mix together
the cream cheese, sugar and vanilla essence or seeds until smooth.
Add the eggs one at a time, mixing thoroughly after each addition.
Scrape down the sides of the bowl to make sure all the ingredients
are mixed through. Fold in the raspberries by hand, then pour the
filling over the biscuit base in the tin.

Place the tin in a deep roasting tray and fill with water until it comes
halfway up the sides of the cake tin. The moisture from this water
bath helps to prevent your cheesecake from cracking and baking too
fast. Bake in the oven for 35–45 minutes, until the cake moves as one
in the middle. Allow the cake to cool in the tin at room temperature,
then place in the fridge for 3–4 hours or overnight.

If you're using gelatine leaves to make the jelly, place them in a bowl of cold water and let it sit for 2 minutes to allow the gelatine to sponge. Remove the gelatine leaves and squeeze out the excess water.

Place the caster sugar and water in a saucepan and bring to a fast boil, stirring continuously to dissolve the sugar. Add the raspberries and return to the boil, then take off the heat. Blitz with a hand-held blender and pour through a fine-mesh sieve into a jug. If you're using powdered gelatine, sprinkle it onto the hot liquid and mix until dissolved, but do not boil. If you have used gelatine sheets, add them to the hot mix at this point and mix well. Add the crème de cassis to taste. Place in the fridge and allow to firm up for about 20 minutes, just until it's a wobbly consistency but not fully set – you still need to be able to pour it over the cheesecake.

Pour the jelly over the cheesecake and allow it to set. Once the jelly is set, remove the cheesecake from the tin and decorate with fresh Chantilly cream and fresh raspberries.

mixed berry white chocolate and almond tart

SERVES 6–8

1 batch of sweet shortcrust pastry
(page 170)

FOR THE FRANGIPANE FILLING:

200g butter, softened

200g icing sugar

200g ground almonds

40g gluten-free plain white flour

4 eggs, separated

700g frozen mixed berries

150g gluten-free white chocolate drops

FOR THE GLAZE:

4 tbsp apricot jam

1 tbsp boiling water

TO SERVE:

fresh cream

crème anglaise (page 179)

vanilla ice cream (page 204)

This particular tart is very adaptable. It looks so attractive once glazed, especially with the mixed berries and white chocolate. Pears poached in red wine and topped with flaked almonds or a simple Bakewell tart are other adaptations of this recipe.

Make the pastry as per the instructions on page 170. Make sure you allow the pastry to rest for at least 1 hour. Use it to line a 27cm flan tin, prod the base all over with a fork and return to the fridge for 15 minutes. You don't need to blind bake the pastry for this recipe.

Preheat the oven to 180°C.

To make the frangipane, cream the butter and icing sugar together in the bowl of a stand mixer using the paddle attachment until light and fluffy. This can take up to 10 minutes.

Mix the ground almonds and plain flour together. Add the egg yolks to the butter mixture along with half of the flour mixture and mix well. Add the egg whites and the remaining flour mixture and mix well again, scraping down the sides of the bowl.

Pour the filling into the pastry case and bake for 25 minutes, until the tart is light golden and firm to the touch. Remove from the oven and cover with the frozen mixed berries and white chocolate drops. Turn off the oven but place the tart back in the oven for 2 minutes to allow the fruit to thaw out. I have to confess that the reason why I turn off the oven at this point is that I have often forgotten that the tart was in there and I end up burning the chocolate. This way, you're only melting it slightly and defrosting the berries.

To glaze, combine the apricot jam with the boiling water and heat in the microwave or in a small saucepan on the hob until it melts. Brush gently onto the tart.

Serve with some fresh cream or crème anglaise and ice cream.

chocolate fondant

SERVES 5 • FOR THE FONDANT:

cocoa powder, for dusting

175g gluten-free dark chocolate drops or bar (70% cocoa solids)

165g butter, plus extra for greasing

6 eggs

215g caster sugar

75g gluten-free plain flour

FOR THE CHOCOLATE GANACHE:

50g cream

250g gluten-free dark chocolate drops (70% cocoa solids)

150g butter, softened and cubed

1 dessertspoon crème de cassis

icing sugar, for dusting

chocolate sauce (use the recipe with the brownies on page 193), to serve

mint ice cream (page 205), to serve

This is a very popular dessert in The Olde Post Inn, as chocoholics adore it. It's very easy to make, but timing is everything and it's best served immediately. It is optional to use the chocolate ganache – the recipe will work fine without it, but be careful of the cooking time, as you want a soft centre.

Grease five dariole moulds or small ramekins with butter, then dust with a little cocoa powder, tapping out any excess.

To make the fondant, chop the chocolate into small pieces if using a bar. Place the chocolate and butter in a heatproof bowl set over a saucepan of gently simmering water, taking care not to let the water touch the bottom of the bowl. Melt slowly, then allow to cool.

Whisk the eggs and sugar together in a large bowl until they reach the ribbon stage, where the mixture holds a figure of eight. Fold in the cooled melted chocolate, then fold in the flour. Refrigerate for at least 2 hours or overnight.

To make the ganache, heat the cream in a saucepan and add the chocolate drops, stirring until smooth. Gradually add the butter cubes, whisking continuously until the ganache is smooth, shiny and glossy. Stir in the crème de cassis at this stage.

Transfer the ganache into a piping bag while it's warm and leave until it starts to set. Line a baking tray with a piece of greaseproof paper and pipe into small 1cm drops onto the paper. Allow to set in the fridge.

Preheat the oven to 180°C.

Pipe or spoon the chocolate fondant mixture into the prepared moulds. Place one chocolate ganache drop into each fondant before baking to add extra richness.

Bake for 8–10 minutes. The fondants should be cooked on the outside but still soft in the centre.

To serve, dust with icing sugar and serve with chocolate sauce and mint ice cream.

GET AHEAD

The ganache drops freeze very well. If not using immediately, freeze them on the baking tray before storing in a ziplock freezer bag. The frozen chocolate ganache drops will last for three months and can be used directly from the freezer.

flourless chocolate torte

MAKES 4 INDIVIDUAL TORTES

125g gluten-free dark chocolate drops (70% cocoa solids)

60g butter, plus extra for greasing

1 shot of espresso (optional)

3 medium eggs, separated

125g caster sugar

vanilla ice cream (page 204) or Chantilly cream, to serve

This chocolate dessert is both rich yet light in texture. The coffee enhances the chocolate flavour. You could make a raspberry torte by placing fresh or frozen raspberries on the base of the dishes and then covering with the chocolate mixture.

Chantilly cream is single cream with icing sugar and vanilla essence or seeds added to taste, then whisked together. It's fantastic with this torte.

Preheat the oven to 160°C. Grease four ramekins.

Place the chocolate and butter in a heatproof bowl set over a saucepan of simmering water, taking care not to let the bottom of the bowl touch the water. Allow the chocolate and butter to melt while stirring continuously, then add the espresso, if using.

Whisk the egg yolks and caster sugar together in a large bowl, then stir in the melted chocolate.

Whisk the egg whites in a spotlessly clean, grease-free bowl to soft peaks. Fold 1 tablespoon of the egg white into the chocolate mix, then gradually fold in the remaining egg white.

Pour the mixture into the greased soufflé dishes and bake for 8 minutes. The tortes will be soft in the centre and crunchy on the outside.

Serve in the soufflé dishes with vanilla ice cream or Chantilly cream.

chocolate fudge cake

SERVES 12

240g light brown Demerara sugar

100g butter, softened, plus extra for greasing

1 tsp vanilla essence

240g gluten-free self-raising flour

40g good-quality cocoa powder

1 tsp bread soda

½ tsp xanthan gum

2 large eggs, separated

140g soured cream

40g gluten-free chocolate drops (70% cocoa solids)

190ml boiling water

1 tsp white wine vinegar

FOR THE FUDGE ICING:

175g chocolate drops (70% cocoa solids)

275g icing sugar

250g butter, softened

1 tsp vanilla essence

FOR THE GANACHE TOPPING:

100g icing sugar, sieved

100g butter

100g gluten-free chocolate drops (70% cocoa solids)

3 tbsp milk

TO ASSEMBLE:

2 tbsp raspberry jam

TO SERVE:

fresh whipped cream

This is the perfect chocolate fudge cake, gluten-free or not!

To prevent the cake mixture from splitting, I always add the egg yolks first to stabilise the mixture and then I gradually add the egg white and flour. This is a foolproof method for any Madeira cake mix.

Preheat the oven to 180°C. Grease 2 x 20cm tins with butter and line with non-stick baking paper.

To make the cake, cream the brown sugar, butter and vanilla essence with the paddle attachment of a food mixer until light and fluffy, stopping to scrape down the sides of the bowl occasionally.

Sieve together the self-raising flour, cocoa power, bread soda and xanthan gum.

Add the egg yolks to the butter and sugar mixture, then add a tablespoon of flour and mix well. Scrape down the sides of the bowl, add one egg white and a tablespoon of flour and mix, once again scraping down the sides of the bowl as you go along. Repeat with the remaining egg white and another tablespoon of flour. Reserve the remaining flour. Add the soured cream and mix to combine.

Place the chocolate drops in a heatproof bowl, pour over the boiling water and mix until all the chocolate is melted before adding the white wine vinegar. Add the melted chocolate to the batter along with the remaining flour and mix through, scraping down the sides of the bowl as you mix.

Divide the batter between the two sponge tins and bake in the oven for 20–25 minutes. The cakes are baked when they are soft to the touch and spring back when gently pressed with a finger. Turn the sponges out onto a wire rack to cool.

To make the fudge icing, melt the chocolate drops in a heatproof bowl set over a saucepan of simmering water, stirring continuously with a spatula and taking care not to let the bottom of the bowl touch the water. Once melted, remove the bowl from the heat and set aside.

Beat the icing sugar and butter together until light and fluffy. Add the melted chocolate and vanilla essence and mix well. To use, place into a piping bag fitted with a star nozzle.

To make the ganache, sieve the icing sugar to remove any lumps. This will result in a smooth, shiny ganache. Place all the ingredients in a bowl set over a saucepan of simmering water, making sure the bottom of the bowl doesn't touch the water. Once the chocolate has melted, remove from the heat and mix well. As it cools it will set and resemble a spread rather than a liquid. You need to use this immediately before it sets fully, so make the ganache just before you assemble the cake.

To assemble, remove the non-stick baking paper from the base of the sponges. Place one sponge on a cake board. Spread with raspberry jam, then spread with a layer of fudge icing and place the other sponge on top. Using a palette knife, spread a light layer of fudge icing on the top and sides of the cake.

To decorate, pipe rosettes of the fudge icing around the top edge of the cake and the base. Pour the chocolate ganache over the top of the cake, letting it run down the sides of the cake. Allow to set for a little while before cutting into slices. Serve with fresh whipped cream.

GET AHEAD

The icing will keep in the fridge for up to seven days. To use, bring back to room temperature so that it's easy to pipe.

chocolate brownies

MAKES 12 LARGE BROWNIES

375g gluten-free dark chocolate drops
(60% cocoa solids)

375g butter

6 eggs

500g caster sugar

175g gluten-free white chocolate
buttons

175g gluten-free self-raising flour

50g coconut flour

FOR THE CHOCOLATE SAUCE:

100g caster sugar

200ml boiling water

200g gluten-free dark chocolate drops
(70% cocoa solids)

*These gorgeous chocolate brownies are gooey in the centre and wonderful
served warm. Instead of white chocolate drops, you can also use dried
cranberries, sour cherries, chopped pecans or chopped hazelnuts.*

Preheat the oven to 180°C. Line a 23cm square baking tin with non-stick
baking paper. Place the chocolate and butter in a heatproof bowl set
over a saucepan of simmering water, making sure the bottom of the bowl
doesn't touch the water, and allow to melt slowly.

Using a whisk attachment on a food mixer, mix the eggs and caster sugar
for approximately 3 minutes, until creamy but not stiff. Mix together the
white chocolate drops, self-raising flour and coconut flour. Combine the
melted chocolate, the egg mixture and the flour mixture and stir well.

Pour into the lined tin and bake for 25 minutes. Reduce the oven
temperature to 100°C and bake for a further 15–20 minutes. To check
if the brownies are baked, give the tin a shake – if there is only a slight
movement on top, then the brownies are done. At this stage the top
should be crusty, but with a gooey centre.

Leave the mixture in the tray overnight, then cut into equal-sized
portions before serving or prior to freezing. The brownies can be stored
for up to four days in an airtight container in the fridge, but remember to
heat gently in a microwave prior to serving.

To make the chocolate sauce, combine the sugar and boiling water in a
saucepan set over a medium heat and stir to dissolve the sugar. Bring to
the boil, then add the chocolate drops and whisk until smooth.

Serve the warm brownies with the chocolate sauce, although the vanilla
ice cream on page 204 or the crème anglaise on page 179 are also good.

GET AHEAD

*The chocolate sauce can be made ahead and reheated as needed. Stored in an airtight
container, it will last for up to four weeks in the fridge. When reheating the chocolate
sauce, it should be done carefully as it can easily burn. The brownies are also suitable for
freezing if you wrap them well individually.*

sticky toffee pudding

SERVES 8–10

175g dark muscovado sugar

75g butter, softened, plus extra for greasing

70g treacle

30g golden syrup

2 eggs, at room temperature

200g gluten-free self-raising flour

200g pitted dates

300ml water

1 tsp bread soda

FOR THE TOFFEE SAUCE:

100g butter

100g dark muscovado sugar

200ml double cream

This recipe is foolproof. It actually works better with gluten-free flour. For the ultimate treat, I like to serve it with the toffee sauce as well as crème anglaise (page 179) or salted caramel ice cream and caramelised banana.

Preheat the oven to 180°C. Grease 8–10 dariole moulds with a little butter.

Using the paddle attachment on a food mixer, cream together the sugar and butter until light and fluffy. This should take about 10 minutes. Scrape down the bowl from time to time to ensure that the mixture is fully combined. Add the treacle and golden syrup and mix well. Add the eggs one a time, mixing well between each addition, then add the flour and mix again, scraping down the sides of the bowl, until all the ingredients are fully combined.

Place the dates in a saucepan with the water and bring to the boil. Immediately remove from the heat and purée the date mixture with a hand-held blender to produce a sloppy mixture. Add the bread soda to the date purée and blend again, then add the date purée to the cake batter and blend well.

Pour the batter into the greased moulds and bake for 20–25 minutes, until the cake shrinks away from the sides of the moulds and springs back when gently pressed with a finger.

While the puddings are baking, you can make the toffee sauce. Melt the butter and sugar together in a saucepan, then add the double cream. Bring to the boil, then reduce the heat and simmer until the mixture coats the back of a spoon. Remove the puddings from the moulds and pour the warm toffee sauce over the puddings to serve.

GET AHEAD

The puddings freeze well. Place in a ziplock bag or sealed container, then freeze. Defrost at room temperature, top with toffee sauce and reheat in a microwave.

tiramisu

MAKES 5 INDIVIDUAL SERVINGS

125ml freshly brewed espresso

2 tbsp Tia Maria

1 tbsp brandy

45g caster sugar, plus extra for sweetening

2 egg yolks

150ml single cream

250g mascarpone cheese

30 amaretti biscuits (page 197)

cocoa powder, for dusting

I love the amaretti biscuit flavour in this recipe. It brings all of the elements together seamlessly. Tiramisu is quite indulgent, but if you're trying to impress, this dessert is guaranteed to do the trick, especially if you serve it in martini glasses, whiskey tumblers or any nice decorative glasses.

If you wish, you can use circles of sponge instead of the amaretti biscuits, especially if you have some stashed in the freezer after making the rhubarb baked Alaska on page 177. Just soak the sponge in the coffee syrup before putting it into the glasses.

Combine the hot coffee with enough sugar to sweeten it. Ensure all the sugar is dissolved before adding the Tia Maria and brandy, then leave to cool.

Place a heatproof bowl over a pan of simmering water. Add the 45g of caster sugar and the egg yolks. Whisk over the heat until they thicken and lighten in colour. If using a thermometer, the mixture will be cooked at 55°C. Remove from the heat and whisk until cold.

Whip the cream in a large bowl to achieve a softly whipped consistency. Add the mascarpone and the cooled egg mixture to the whipped cream. Whisk until all the ingredients are combined, you have achieved a smooth consistency and the mixture holds its shape. Place in a piping bag.

Layer the glasses by first crushing the amaretti biscuits and adding some to the bottom of the serving glasses. Add a dessertspoon of the coffee mixture on top of the biscuits, then pipe in some of the cream mixture. Repeat the layers until you reach the top of the glass, finishing with the cream. Dust with cocoa powder and serve.

amaretti biscuits

MAKES 100 SMALL BISCUITS

2 egg whites (60g egg whites)

150g caster sugar

120g ground almonds

15g gluten-free plain flour

15g cornflour

1 tsp ground cinnamon

icing sugar, for dusting

These biscuits can be used in the tiramisu on page 196 or on their own with a cup of coffee.

Preheat the oven to 180°C. Line a baking tray with non-stick baking paper or a silicone baking mat.

Whisk the egg whites in a spotlessly clean, grease-free bowl until stiff. Gradually add 75g of the caster sugar and whisk until the meringue is dry and glossy.

Sieve together the remaining 75g of caster sugar with the ground almonds, flour, cornflour and cinnamon. Gradually fold the dry mixture into the meringue. Spoon into a piping bag fitted with a plain nozzle and pipe into small balls on the lined tray. Dust liberally with icing sugar and set aside for 1 hour at room temperature before baking. This helps to form a skin on the biscuit.

Bake for 15–20 minutes, until the biscuits are firm and they lift easily from the tray. Allow to cool directly on the tray, then store in an airtight container for two to three weeks.

black forest trifle

SERVES 8–10 • FOR THE CHOCOLATE ROULADE:

sunflower oil, for greasing

5 eggs, separated

175g caster sugar

175g gluten-free dark chocolate drops (70% cocoa solids)

70ml boiling water

FOR THE CHERRY FILLING:

1 x 425g tin of black cherries, pitted

60ml kirsch

45g caster sugar

zest and juice of 1 orange

3 dessertspoons cornflour

1 batch of crème anglaise (page 179)

TO DECORATE:

whipped cream

gluten-free chocolate shavings

This classic dessert consists of a layer of chocolate roulade with cherry compote, crème anglaise, whipped cream and chocolate shavings all presented in a glass serving dish. The layers of texture and colour is quite impressive.

First drain the cherries and reserve the liquid. Soak the cherries in the kirsch for about 30 minutes.

Preheat the oven to 180°C. Line a Swiss roll tin (30cm x 20cm) with non-stick baking paper and brush the paper with a little sunflower oil.

To make the chocolate roulade, place the egg yolks and sugar in the bowl of a stand mixer. Use the balloon whisk attachment to beat the mixture until it's light and fluffy, stopping to scrape down the sides of the bowl occasionally.

Place the chocolate drops in a heatproof bowl and pour over the boiling water. Mix the drops until they are melted and smooth.

Whisk the egg whites in a spotlessly clean, grease-free bowl until they form soft peaks. Do not overmix the whites at this point.

Add the melted chocolate to the egg yolk mixture and stir to combine. Gently fold in a small amount of the egg white, then add the remainder of the egg whites and carefully combine. Pour the mixture into the baking tray and spread out evenly with a spatula or palette knife. Bake in the oven for 12 minutes. The roulade is baked once it has a crust and is firm to touch. However, do not overcook as it could dry out quite easily.

Remove from the oven and leave to cool in the tin, then turn out onto a board and peel off the paper. Using a round 5cm cutter, stamp out into discs.

To make the cherry filling, strain the kirsch from the cherries into a saucepan. Add the reserved cherry liquid from the tin, the sugar and the orange zest and juice. Place the cornflour in a cup, add 1 tablespoon of the liquid from the saucepan and stir to combine. Bring the liquid in the saucepan to the boil, then add the cornflour mixture and cook for 1–2 minutes, stirring continuously. When the liquid has thickened, reduce the heat and simmer for 2 minutes. Add the cherries and set aside to cool.

To assemble, place a circle of roulade in the base of each individual trifle dish. Place a dessertspoon of the cherry filling on top and add a layer of crème anglaise. Repeat the layers. To finish, pipe a rosette or quenelle of whipped cream on top of the trifle and scatter with chocolate shavings. To complete, add a cherry on top.

pavlova nests

MAKES 8 • FOR THE PAVLOVA NESTS:

4 egg whites, at room temperature

225g caster sugar

1½ tsp cornflour

1½ tsp white wine vinegar

FOR THE FILLING:

250ml cream, whipped

1 dessertspoon icing sugar, sieved

1 vanilla pod, split in half and seeds scraped out, or ½ tsp vanilla essence

fresh fruit, to serve (see the recipe intro)

Pavlova nests are crisp on the outside with a soft, marshmallow-light centre. When served with seasonal fruits, it can be a real showstopper. I use fresh mixed berries in the summertime, while figs and toasted almonds or poached pears and toasted pistachios are wonderful combinations in the autumn or winter.

Preheat the oven to 100°C.

It's very important that you use a spotlessly clean, dry, grease-free bowl for whisking the egg whites. You will never achieve the required volume in your pavlova if there is any trace of grease in the mixture. You can also achieve good volume by having your eggs at room temperature. Clean your whisk attachment and mixing bowl with boiling water before use and dry well. I use kitchen paper to wipe the bowl and attachment.

Using the balloon whisk attachment of a stand mixer, whisk the egg whites until they are foamy and maintain soft peaks. Gradually add the caster sugar one spoonful at a time, mixing well after each spoonful. When all the sugar has been added, mix on high speed for 3–4 minutes. The biggest mistake people make when making pavlova or meringues is under-mixing, which will result in the pavlova not holding its shape. It is impossible to overmix.

Mix the cornflour and white wine vinegar to a paste in a cup, then add to the meringue and mix well to fully combine.

Place a tiny drop of the meringue on the reverse side corners of non-stick baking paper to hold the paper in place on the baking tray (alternatively, you can use a silicone baking mat). Put six to eight separate dollops of the meringue onto the lined tray, making a slight hollow in the centre using the back of the spoon. This will hold the fresh cream and fruit when baked.

Bake for 80 minutes, then leave the tray in the oven, turn the oven off and leave the door open to allow the nests to dry out and cool.

To make the cream filling, combine the cream, icing sugar and vanilla in a bowl. Whip together until the mixture holds its shape and can be piped or placed in the centre of the pavlova nests. Top with the fresh fruit.

GET AHEAD

The nests can be made two or three days ahead of time and assembled when needed.

olde post inn vanilla crème brûlée

SERVES 4

500ml single cream

50g icing sugar

½ vanilla pod, split in half and seeds scraped out

5 egg yolks

light brown Demerara sugar, for caramelising

fresh seasonal berries, to serve

This is a favourite of our customers in The Olde Post Inn. Traditionally we serve it with seasonal berries and the ginger shortbread biscuits on page 220.

Preheat the oven to 100°C.

To make the custard, place the cream and 25g of the icing sugar in a large saucepan along with the vanilla seeds and bring to the boil. Remove from the heat and set aside.

Mix the egg yolks and the remaining 25g of icing sugar together in a large heatproof bowl. Pour the hot cream into the egg yolks and whisk well.

Pour the custard through a fine-mesh sieve to remove the vanilla pod and any lumps and to ensure that you have a smooth custard. Pour equal portions of the custard into four ramekins or shallow ovenproof serving dishes.

Place the dishes in a roasting tin and pour in enough water to come halfway up the sides of the dishes. Transfer to the oven and bake for 20–30 minutes. The cooking time will vary depending on how deep your dishes are. The crème brûlée is baked when it wobbles slightly as a whole. Allow to cool, then place in the fridge until chilled.

Before serving, sprinkle with the Demerara sugar and caramelise with a kitchen blowtorch or under a hot grill. This results in a light sheet of caramel. Repeat the process three times to get a really good crust on the custard. Top with fresh seasonal berries and serve immediately.

GET AHEAD

This dessert can be prepared in advance and kept in the fridge overnight. To serve, simply remove from the fridge, glaze and serve immediately.

vanilla ice cream

MAKES 1.5 LITRES

1 litre full-fat milk

250ml single cream

1 vanilla pod

13 egg yolks

275g caster sugar

There is nothing like homemade ice cream. It is absolutely worth the effort and time.

Place the milk and cream in a large heavy-based saucepan. It's important to use a large saucepan to allow the milk and cream to rise and triple in size as it cooks. Cut the vanilla pod in half and scrape out the seeds. Add the seeds and the pod to the pan. Bring the mix up to a very good boil that is rising up the sides of the pan. This will ensure that the custard is almost cooked already so that it won't take long to attain the correct consistency at the next stage.

Whisk the egg yolks and caster sugar together in a heatproof bowl until fully combined. Add the boiling liquid to the egg mixture and whisk immediately to prevent it from curdling. Pour the mixture back into the saucepan through a fine-mesh sieve and place it back on the heat, whisking continuously, until it coats the back of a spoon. This should only take 1 minute.

Once cool, place the custard into an ice cream machine and churn according to the manufacturer's instructions.

mint ice cream

MAKES 750ML

20 fresh mint leaves

40ml crème de menthe

½ x vanilla ice cream recipe (page 204)

This ice cream is wonderful with the chocolate fondant on page 186.

Have a basin of ice-cold water ready. Bring a small pot of water to the boil. Blanch the mint leaves by placing them into the boiling water for 10 seconds, then remove and refresh in the iced water. Pat dry using kitchen paper.

Blitz the mint in a blender, then add the crème de menthe and blitz again. Add the mint mixture to the vanilla ice cream to taste and churn to combine.

afternoon tea

AFTERNOON TEA is cooler than ever, but
for those of us who are coeliac, it's simply
a nightmare. I would like to change that!

victoria sponge

MAKES 2 x 20CM SPONGES

butter, for greasing

6 medium eggs, at room temperature

180g caster sugar

140g gluten-free self-raising flour

40g gluten-free cornflour

This traditional sponge can be a component of many desserts or it can simply be served on its own with fresh cream and jam.

Preheat the oven to 180°C. Grease 2 x 20cm sandwich tins with a little butter and line the bases with non-stick baking paper.

Whisk the eggs and caster sugar together until you can form a peak with the whisk and it holds a figure of eight. This should take about 10 minutes. It helps to have the eggs at room temperature in order to achieve this.

Sieve the self-raising flour and the cornflour together, then gently fold into the egg mixture until just combined. Do not overmix.

Pour into the prepared tins and bake for 25–30 minutes, until the sponges shrink from the sides of the tin and spring back when gently pressed with a finger. The mixture will double in volume when baked.

GET AHEAD

You can make these sponges in advance and freeze them once they are well wrapped.

pear and almond scones

A delicious twist to a traditional scone.

MAKES 10 SCONES

150g gluten-free self-raising flour

150g gluten-free white flour blend

1 tsp gluten-free baking powder

½ tsp xanthan gum

½ tsp bread soda

½ tsp salt

40g caster sugar, plus extra for sprinkling

70g butter, cubed

1 egg

200ml buttermilk approximately

FOR THE FRANGIPANE FILLING:

200g butter, softened

200g icing sugar

200g ground almonds

40g gluten-free plain white flour, plus extra for dusting

4 eggs, separated

1 x 400g tin of pears, drained and sliced

flaked almonds, to decorate

Preheat the oven to 180°C. Dust a non-stick baking tray with a little gluten-free plain white flour.

To make the frangipane, cream the butter and icing sugar together in the bowl of a stand mixer using the paddle attachment until light and fluffy. This can take up to 10 minutes.

Mix the ground almonds and plain flour together. Add the egg yolks to the butter mixture along with half of the flour mixture and mix well. Add the egg whites and the remaining flour mixture and mix well again, scraping down the sides of the bowl. Put the frangipane mixture into a piping bag and set aside.

To make the scones, sieve all the dry ingredients together except the sugar, then mix in the sugar and rub in the butter until it's a sandy texture. Make a well in the centre.

Whisk the egg and reserve a tablespoon of the egg to use later. Mix the remainder of the egg with 150ml of the buttermilk, then gently mix into the flour mixture until it's incorporated. If the dough is not bound together yet, then add the rest of the buttermilk, little by little, until you achieve the required consistency.

Transfer the dough onto a floured board and pat down until it's 3cm thick. Gentle handling is essential to produce a light scone. Use a 4cm scone cutter to stamp out the scones. Place the scones on the prepared baking tray.

Pipe a small ball of frangipane into the centre of each scone and place a slice of pear on top of each one. Brush the scones with the reserved tablespoon of beaten egg and sprinkle with caster sugar and some flaked almonds.

Place in the oven, then immediately reduce the temperature to 160°C and bake for 20–25 minutes, until the scones are well risen, golden brown and firm to the touch. Transfer to a wire rack and leave to cool.

GET AHEAD

Freeze whatever frangipane you don't use to make another batch of scones on another day, as you only use a small amount in this recipe.

carrot cake

MAKES 2 X 1LB LOAVES

125g gluten-free self-raising flour

2 tsp gluten-free baking powder

1 tsp ground cinnamon

1 tsp salt

125g gluten-free brown bread flour

175g caster sugar

150ml sunflower oil

4 eggs

350g carrots, grated

100g walnuts, roughly chopped

FOR THE ICING:

300g icing sugar, sieved

125g cream cheese

50g butter, softened

zest of 1 orange

1 drop of vanilla essence

I have a sweet tooth, so a slice of this cake with a cup of coffee in the afternoon is just perfect. The cake has a soft, dense texture, flavoured by the addition of the cinnamon.

Preheat the oven to 180°C. Line 2 x 1lb loaf tins with non-stick baking paper.

Sieve the self-raising flour, baking powder, cinnamon and salt together in a bowl, then stir in the brown bread flour.

Whisk the caster sugar, sunflower oil and eggs together in a large bowl until it forms a batter. Add the flour mixture to the batter, then add the grated carrots and chopped walnuts. Mix until combined.

Pour into the loaf tins and bake for 50–60 minutes, until the cake springs back when you touch it. Allow the cakes to cool completely on a wire rack before icing them.

To make the icing, cream the icing sugar, cream cheese, butter, orange zest and vanilla essence together until it forms a smooth icing. Spread over the cooled cakes with a spatula.

GET AHEAD

The cake freezes well prior to icing.

basic cupcakes

MAKES 12 CUPCAKES

125g butter, softened

125g caster sugar

2 eggs, separated

½ tsp vanilla essence or the seeds from 1 vanilla pod

125g gluten-free self-raising flour

15g cornflour

½ tsp xanthan gum

This basic mix is moist and light and is good for making all types of cupcakes.

Preheat the oven to 180°C. Line a bun tray with cases.

Using the paddle attachment on your food mixer, cream the butter and sugar together until light and fluffy. This should take approximately 10 minutes. Add the egg yolks one at a time, mixing well between each addition, then add the vanilla.

Sieve the flour, cornflour and xanthan gum together to remove any lumps. Add one spoonful of the egg whites and one spoonful of the flour mixture to the butter mixture and combine well. Repeat the process until everything is combined.

Put the mixture into the bun cases using a spoon or piping bag and bake for 20 minutes. Allow to cool completely before icing with one of the toppings on pages 216–217.

GET AHEAD

The baked cupcakes freeze very well, so I recommend doubling this recipe. The cupcakes defrost relatively quickly when needed.

tiramisu cupcakes

MAKES ENOUGH FOR 12 CUPCAKES

250ml freshly brewed espresso

1 tbsp caster sugar

80ml Tia Maria

10ml brandy

200g mascarpone cheese

150ml single cream

1 batch of basic cupcakes (page 214)

1 tbsp cocoa powder, for dusting

gluten-free chocolate shavings, to decorate

Combine the hot coffee with the caster sugar. Ensure all the sugar has dissolved before adding the Tia Maria and brandy. Leave to cool.

Using an electric whisk, mix the mascarpone cheese and the single cream together until they hold soft peaks.

Cut a small hole in the top of each baked cupcake and pour in some of the coffee mixture. Replace the top of the cupcake, then pipe the icing on top. Dust with cocoa power and decorate with chocolate shavings.

walnut and honey cupcakes

MAKES ENOUGH FOR 12 CUPCAKES

250g icing sugar, sieved

125g butter, softened

½ tsp vanilla essence

50g full-fat cream cheese

1 tbsp single cream

2 tsp honey

1 batch of basic cupcakes (page 214)

50g walnuts, chopped

Cream the icing sugar, butter and vanilla essence together. Add the cream cheese, cream and honey and whisk until light and fluffy. Place in a piping bag and pipe onto the baked cupcakes. Decorate the cupcakes with the chopped walnuts.

lemon meringue cupcakes

Only make the meringue when the cupcakes are ready for use, as it needs to be used straight away for a good result.

MAKES ENOUGH FOR 12 CUPCAKES 1 BATCH OF BASIC CUPCAKES (PAGE 214) • FOR THE LEMON CURD:

1 leaf of gelatine or 1 tsp powdered gelatine

175g caster sugar

5 eggs

125ml single cream

zest and juice of 3 lemons

FOR THE MERINGUE:

3 egg whites (100g)

150g caster sugar

icing sugar, for dusting

To make the lemon curd, soak the gelatine leaf, if using, in a bowl of cold water. Mix the sugar, eggs and cream together, then whisk in the lemon zest and juice. Transfer to a saucepan and bring to the boil over a medium heat, stirring continuously. Remove from the heat, add the soaked gelatine leaf or powdered gelatine and leave to dissolve. Once cool, spoon the lemon curd into a piping bag and set aside.

To make the meringue, use the balloon whisk attachment on your mixer to whip the egg whites to soft peaks. Gradually add the caster sugar, whisking on a high speed until it's stiff and glossy. This should take about 10 minutes. You can use a piping bag with a nozzle to pipe the meringue onto the curd.

To assemble, preheat the oven to 180°C. Cut into the centre of each cupcake with a pointed knife, removing a small amount of the bun. Pipe in about 1 teaspoon of the curd and replace the cupcake top. Once all the cupcakes have been filled, pipe the meringue onto each one, finishing with a dramatic swirl. Dust with icing sugar and bake in the oven for 4–5 minutes, until the top is set and slightly coloured.

GET AHEAD

This makes more lemon curd than you will need for the cupcakes, but it keeps for up to two weeks in a sealed container in the fridge. Or you could use it in combination with whipped cream for a lemon curd pavlova using the recipe for pavlova nests on page 198.

emma's chocolate chip cookies

MAKES 30–40 COOKIES

225g butter, softened

150g Demerara sugar

100g coconut palm sugar or caster sugar

½ tsp vanilla essence or the seeds of 1 vanilla pod

2 eggs, separated

300g gluten-free self-raising flour

50g coconut flour

1 tsp bread soda

½ tsp gluten-free baking powder

½ tsp xanthan gum

pinch of salt

125g gluten-free white chocolate drops

125g gluten-free dark chocolate drops

My daughter Emma cannot resist these and plagues me to make them. This cookie recipe may look like it has a lot of ingredients, but once the raw cookie dough is rolled in cling film and refrigerated, it will keep in the fridge until required for up to one week. These are very popular in my house, especially for parties. They have a lovely short texture and are very satisfying.

Preheat the oven to 180°C.

Using the paddle attachment of your food mixer, cream the butter, Demerara sugar and coconut palm sugar together until the mixture is light and fluffy. This should take about 10 minutes. Mix in the vanilla, then add the egg yolks and mix well to combine.

Sieve the self-raising flour, coconut flour, bread soda, baking powder, xanthan gum and a pinch of salt together.

Add half the egg whites and half the flour mixture to the butter and sugar mixture and mix until the egg whites and flour are fully combined with the butter mix, scraping down the sides of the bowl during the process. Add the remaining egg white and flour and mix again, then add the chocolate drops and mix through.

Break off a heaped dessertspoon of the dough and place on a non-stick baking tray. Bake for 8–10 minutes, depending on the size. The cookies will be light brown in colour when baked. Remove from the oven and allow to cool directly on the tray. You can store the cookies for up to a week in an airtight container.

GET AHEAD

If you want to use the dough later, then form it into a cylinder, wrap it tightly in cling film and place in the fridge until required. The dough will keep for up to a week. Or you can freeze it and defrost it when required. Either way, slice the dough into 1cm-thick circles to bake.

ginger shortbread biscuits

MAKES 12–15

200g gluten-free plain white flour

150g butter, softened

75g caster sugar, plus extra for dusting

1 vanilla pod, split in half and seeds scraped out

40g crystallised ginger, chopped

Real butter brings out the flavour of these biscuits, which are the perfect accompaniment to a cup of coffee or served alongside the crème brûlée on page 203 or a trifle. I enjoy making these biscuits with the children, as they can be decorated with icing. You can also use chopped pistachios or the zest of one lemon instead of the crystallised ginger.

Preheat the oven to 160°C. Line a baking tray with non-stick baking paper.

Mix the flour, butter, sugar and vanilla seeds together to form a crumb mix. Add the chopped ginger and bring together to form a dough. Roll into a cylinder and cut into 1cm-thick circles. Place on the lined baking tray.

Bake for 20–25 minutes, until the biscuits are firm to the touch and pale in colour. Leave to cool directly on the tray and dust with caster sugar until fully covered.

Store the biscuits in an airtight container and use within a week.

conversion charts

Oven temperatures

Celcius	Fahrenheit	Gas
110°C	225°F	¼
120°C	250°F	½
140°C	275°F	1
150°C	300°F	2
160°C	325°F	3
170°C	325°F	3
180°C	350°F	4
190°C	375°F	5
200°C	400°F	6
220°C	425°F	7
230°C	450°F	8

Volume

Metric	Imperial	Metric	Imperial	Metric	Imperial
25ml	1fl oz	300ml	10fl oz	1 litre	1¼ pints
50ml	2fl oz	350ml	12fl oz	1.2 litres	2 pints
75ml	2½fl oz	400ml	14fl oz	1.3 litres	2¼ pints
100ml	3½fl oz	425ml	15fl oz	1.4 litres	2½ pints
125ml	4fl oz	450ml	16fl oz	1.5 litres	2¾ pints
150ml	5fl oz	500ml	18fl oz	1.7 litres	3 pints
175ml	6fl oz	568ml	20fl oz	2 litres	3½ pints
200ml	7fl oz	600ml	1 pint	2.5 litres	4½ pints
225ml	8fl oz	700ml	1¼ pints	2.8 litres	5 pints
250ml	9fl oz	850ml	1½ pints	3 litres	5¼ pints

Weight

Metric	Imperial		Metric	Imperial
5g	⅛ oz		325g	11½oz
10g	¼oz		350g	12oz
15g	½oz		375g	13oz
20g	¾oz		00g	14oz
25g	1oz		425g	15oz
35g	1¼oz		450g	1lb
40g	1½oz		500g	1lb 2oz
50g	1¾oz		550g	1lb 4oz
55g	2oz		600g	1lb 5oz
60g	2¼oz		650g	1lb 7oz
70g	2½oz		700g	1lb 9oz
75g	2¾oz		750g	1lb 10oz
85g	3oz		800g	1lb 12oz
90g	3¼oz		850g	1lb 14oz
100g	3½oz		900g	2lb
115g	4oz		950g	2lb 2oz
125g	4½oz		1kg	2lb 4oz
140g	5oz		1.25kg	2lb 12oz
150g	5½oz		1.3kg	3lb
175g	6oz		1.5kg	3lb 5oz
200g	7oz		1.6kg	3lb 8oz
225g	8oz		1.8kg	4lb
250g	9oz		2kg	4lb 8oz
275g	9¾oz		2.25kg	5lb
280g	10oz		2.5kg	5lb 8oz
300g	10½oz		.7kg	6lb
315g	11oz		3kg	6lb 8oz

Spoons

Metric	Imperial
1.25ml	¼ tsp
2.5ml	½ tsp
5ml	1 tsp
10ml	2 tsp
15ml	3 tsp/1 tbsp
30ml	2 tbsp
45ml	3 tbsp
60ml	4 tbsp
75ml	5 tbsp
90ml	6 tbsp

US cups

cups	Metric
¼ cup	60ml
⅓ cup	70ml
½ cup	125ml
⅔ cup	150ml
¾ cup	175ml
1 cup	250ml
1½ cups	375ml
2 cups	500ml
3 cups	750ml
4 cups	1 litre

index

u
ultimate burger, 117, 119
US cups, 225

v
vanilla crème brûlée, 203
vanilla ice cream, 204
Victoria sponge, 208
vinaigrette, 110–111
volume, 223

w
walnut and honey cupcakes, 216
weight, 224
Welsh rarebit with mushrooms, 24
white bean and sausage casserole, 80
white pudding, 26–27
white wine cream, 72
wild garlic pesto, 166
wild garlic pesto bread, 37
Worcestershire sauce, xxiv

x
xanthan gum, xxi

y
Yorkshire pudding, 114–115